Dear Parent,

Thank you for subscribing to PARENTING magazine. This copy of **The New Mother's Body** is your free gift. I hope that both PARENTING and **The New Mother's Body** prove to be enjoyable and valuable resources for you as a new parent.

If you have any questions about your subscription, please write us at:

PARENTING
P.O. Box 56861
Boulder, CO 80322-6861

Or, call our toll-free subscriber hotline:
1-800-234-0847.

Sincerely,

Robin Wolaner
Publisher

P.S.: For information on ordering gifts and additional subscriptions, see the following page.

PARENTING

SHARE PARENTING WITH A FRIEND

Cut out this form and give it to a friend — they can order one year of PARENTING magazine (10 issues) for only $12—a savings of 33% off the regular price.

☐ **YES,** Send me a year of PARENTING at 33% off

NAME _____

ADDRESS _____

CITY/STATE/ZIP _____

For PARENTING gift subscription orders, complete the section below. You'll receive a handsome gift card to personally sign and send to your gift recipient. Each gift costs only $12.

Send a one-year gift subscription to:

NAME _____

ADDRESS _____

CITY/STATE/ZIP _____

Send the invoice and gift announcement card to:

NAME _____

ADDRESS _____

CITY/STATE/ZIP _____

Return this form to: PARENTING   5NMB
                         P.O. Box 56861
                         Boulder, CO 80322-6861

THE NEW MOTHER'S BODY

A COMPLETE GUIDE TO THE FIRST YEAR POSTPARTUM

by Paula M. Siegel

Foreword by Shelley Kolton, M.D.

Illustrated by Sharon D. Siegel

BANTAM BOOKS
NEW YORK · TORONTO · LONDON · SYDNEY · AUCKLAND

This book is not intended as a substitute for medical advice of physicians. The reader should regularly consult a physician in matters relating to his or her health and particularly in respect of any symptoms which may require diagnosis or medical attention.

THE NEW MOTHER'S BODY
A Bantam Book / July 1988

ISBN 0-553-26899-6

Published simultaneously in the United States and Canada

Bantam Books are published by Bantam Books, a division of Bantam Doubleday Dell Publishing Group, Inc. Its trademark, consisting of the words "Bantam Books" and the portrayal of a rooster, is Registered in U.S. Patent and Trademark Office and in other countries. Marca Registrada. Bantam Books, 666 Fifth Avenue, New York, New York 10103.

PRINTED IN THE UNITED STATES OF AMERICA

O   0 9 8 7 6 5 4 3 2

For my mother, Gladys Goldman Siegel, whose delight in life, spirit of adventure, and innate generosity continue to inspire me.

I'd like to thank Shelley Kolton, MD, for her guidance and cooperation in this project, as well as Nancy Kraus, CNM, and Jo Leonard, RN, for sharing their insights into the postpartum recovery process. The American College of Obstetrics and Gynecology also provided me with valuable information and suggestions for further research. And I am especially grateful to all of the mothers who took the time to share their postpartum experiences with me.

Once again, I want to express my gratitude to my agent and guiding light, Janet Manus, whose pushing and cajoling gives me the confidence to pursue greater goals. I also want to thank Susan Marcus Palau for bringing me into the fold of new mothers and for enriching my life with her friendship, and my sister Sharon for her sensitive and illuminating illustrations.

Finally, I owe thanks Herminia and Chevere Resto whose dependability and devotion to my son allow me to work without worry or guilt.

CONTENTS

PART 2: THE FIRST SIX WEEKS

PART 3: SIX WEEKS TO THREE MONTHS

PART 4: FOUR TO TWELVE MONTHS

FOREWORD

Quietness is most desirable during the first week, and the visits of friends, except those necessary for the comfort of the patient, should not be allowed. All mental excitement is apt to be very injurious. Until the eighth or tenth day, at least, the patient must not leave her bed for any purpose. While the bed is being made, she should be covered with a blanket, and if the lower sheet requires to be changed, she is to be gently rolled first to one side and then to the other." (A. Donald, *An Introduction to Midwifery: A Handbook for Medical Students and Midwives*, 1894) Imagine Dr. Donald's chagrin if his "lying-in woman" were to sit up in bed and demand that he explain to her *why* her stitches were burning, her hemorrhoids aching, her uterus cramping, and her breasts engorged beyond the limits of her only brassiere.

Although medical knowledge and women's independence have come an equally long and impressive distance since 1894, both are in the early stages of tremendous growth. And as the field of obstetrics explodes with new understanding and capabilities, women must prepare to amass this information on their own terms, in order to participate intelligently in their own care and to regain the control that is rightfully theirs in the process of childbirth. This responsibility may seem awesome to many a woman who has already pushed herself to be productive at work or at home or both and secretly wishes that after the baby is born she too could be a lying-in woman. But it is women and not their physicians who have strived for a more flexible and active role, both during and after pregnancy, in part because they wanted it and in part because they needed it to survive professionally in their struggle for equality at work.

Women's health care has seen extraordinary changes over the past twenty years, largely due to two factors. Women, faced with stifling, sexual stereotypes, found it necessary to gather and use as much factual information about their bodies and their health care as possible—their self-education was truly remarkable. Secondly, obstetrician-gynecologists were more responsive to this demand for knowledge from their patients than any other group of physicians in modern times. The dialogue between the two has been constant and often exhausting, but the change, albeit only a beginning, has been most encouraging.

The postpartum period today marks the modern mother's most challenging transition. No longer is her care and her behavior so rigidly prescribed as to preclude choices. The decisions she makes during this time are complex: they involve her work and her partner, her child and his or her care, her identity in the past and her aspirations for the future. It is a time made easier by understanding: Understanding the physical changes that every woman awakens to *after* the baby is born. Understanding what is normal and what is not, what will be temporary and what may last forever. Understanding how to move ahead gracefully when faced with a new life that is both wonderful and scary.

Paula Siegel has given every woman the opportunity to master this transition with this excellent book, *The New Mother's Body*. With sensitivity and humor she takes every woman through the aches and pains, the joys and the blues, of new motherhood. The book is remarkably nonjudgmental; each woman will be able to find herself somewhere in the pages and feel taken care of. It is organized chronologically, taking the reader from those first moments after birth through the first year; a final chapter is added for those energetic and ambitious mothers who are readying themselves for another pregnancy. Ms Siegel has included an excellent section for women having Cesarean sections, chapters on diet and weight loss, sex and exercise, which are supportive, realistic and medically sound.

Although most women in labor are not thinking about their postpartum period, I would recommend that Paula Siegel's book accompany them to their delivery. They will find it a wonderful resource for their first days of motherhood, with answers to all of their questions about nursing, episiotomy pain, bleeding, uterine cramps . . . the list goes on. Physicians and midwives will be delighted to have such assistance in the care of their patients.

—Shelley Kolton, M.D.

INTRODUCTION

When I went into the hospital to give birth to my son, I carefully chose the clothes I'd wear home. They had to be comfortable but could not be maternity wear. I picked out a pair of jeans that were baggy on me before I was pregnant and a loose-fitting shirt. From the little I found to read about the first few days postpartum, I knew that I wouldn't fit back into my old clothes immediately, nor would I want to fuss with stockings and skirt.

What I didn't know was that putting on jeans after having a healthy-sized episiotomy during birth was a torture tailor-made for a new mother. Just trying to get my feet through the legs of the pants made me grimace with discomfort. Gratefully, I slid into the dress I wore when I checked into the labor room and waddled out to the car. In the back of my mind on the way home, I harbored the thought that my doctor hadn't put me back together properly. After all, it had been late. She'd looked tired. Nobody had told me to expect this raw pain between my legs, and they'd told me about every other discomfort I could expect. Something had to be wrong. I resigned myself to the fact that I was one of those unlucky few who fell through the safety net and were irreparably damaged.

Of course, that wasn't the case. My doctor's surgical skills are admirable. A year later, I couldn't remember what the incision felt like. My problem at the time was that I didn't know what to expect in the first few days and weeks of my postpartum recovery. On account of my ignorance, I didn't soak in a sitz bath as often as I should have to soothe the incision. I didn't know about the local topical anesthetic available just for the asking. And most importantly, I was afraid that something was wrong, and my fear heightened the discomfort I felt from the episiotomy.

Many of us expect to be efficient mothers, spirited and content, the day we walk out of the hospital. We're concerned, then, to find ourselves still feeling the soreness of delivery incisions, still in an emotional tangle over our new babies, our work and our partners, and still looking pear-shaped and bloated several weeks after birth.

Compounding this unexpected lingering of postpartum effects is the sudden independence from the close medical monitoring we'd experienced during pregnancy. For nine months every physical change was measured and managed. We grew used to the regular feedback from the doctor assuaging our fears about aches, cravings and moods, as well as to reinforcing that sense of security by referring to our library of books on childbearing that discussed every physical change and psychological nuance of pregnancy. Now, however, with the exception of a brief six-week checkup, we are left on our own to cope with our recovery as well as with the demanding job of motherhood. And while endless experts have written down their advice on caring for the new family member and the emotional aspects of motherhood, few have been moved to advise the mother on how to handle her *physical* recovery.

I found my first source of information about postpartum recovery in a nearby playground where new mothers were lined up one carriage after another on the "nursing" bench. I took the last seat and proceeded to cover myself with a blanket, unbutton my sundress, and try to get my baby on the breast without exposing myself. After much fumbling and perspiring in the 100° heat, I was just getting settled when the mother to my left turned to see who the newcomer was. "Oh my God," she said, pushing the blanket away from Willie's face and, of course, leaving me exposed to passers-by, "are you trying to smother him?" At first I was taken aback by this stranger undoing my carefully arranged cover, but I saw she was smiling and nursing her own baby under the small but effective cover of a jersey shirt. "You should try wearing a blouse or shirt," Susan said. "You just lift it up. It covers you and the baby and it's much easier than erecting a tent like that every time you want to nurse."

My bench friend was the mother of a baby three months older than mine. Those extra three months made her an authority not only in the area of nursing but in postpartum bleeding, emotional difficulties, sleep deprivation, and sexual relationships. She was my pospartum Dr. Spock. During our mornings in the park, Susan helped me realize that I was not alone in feeling sluggish and fat, that all the women on the bench had some postpartum problem they hadn't expected, and that in my own time I would find a way to make motherhood the part of my life I wanted it to be.

Most new mothers depend, as I did, on advice from neighbors, sisters, aunts, and friends due to the dearth of information about physical recovery after birth. Unfortunately, this advice can be as harmful as it is helpful, just as it was during pregnancy. It's great for the new mother if a more experienced woman can lessen her doubts and fears. However, too often the advice only intensifies worries. A well-meaning mother who was taught that bottle-feeding was more reliable than breastfeeding might make her daughter feel insecure about her milk supply. A friend who lost all of her weight quickly might make another woman feel guilty about her slow weight loss.

What we need in our early months of mothering is a guide to help us understand the range of normal postpartum experiences. After all, what is normal for a new mother in the first few weeks following childbirth would be considered a medical emergency in any other circumstance.

- Many women lose fifteen or more pounds during delivery, and then drop another ten or so in the first few weeks after birth as the body rids itself of accumulated water. The combined loss might approach 20 or 25 percent of total body weight in as little as two or three weeks.
- Blood volume, which increased by 40 percent during pregnancy, drops precipitously after birth and returns to its normal level in just a week.
- Hormonal changes also are remarkable. Once the placenta is delivered, the level of estrogen in the body immediately

plummets and may not return to normal for a few weeks or until the menstrual cycle returns. The dramatic drop often affects moods, sexual desire, and sexual response.

Very few of us are prepared for the enormity of the normal changes in our bodies immediately after birth. At the same time that we want to put aside our needs to nurture our newborn, we often are unhappily surprised by our own physical disabilities. Certainly, some information about coping with our own physical healing following birth would allow us to be better prepared to meet both our newborns' and our own needs at the same time. *The New Mother's Body* was written to provide information that would ease the mother's and the newborn's abrupt introduction to a new life.

Most books on pregnancy point to the fact that each pregnancy and childbirth experience is different from the next—even for the same woman. The same is true of the postpartum experience. It will vary from one woman to another, and even from one baby to the next in the same woman. In this book you'll find an overview of the wide variety of symptoms experienced by healthy postpartum women. Not all of these aftereffects of birth will be experienced by every woman. This extensive coverage of physical changes after birth is meant less as a prediction of what an individual woman will feel than as a reference that every woman can use to find practical advice to make her entrance into motherhood more graceful and less trying. It is my hope that *The New Mother's Body* will fill the gap in your library between your childbirth and childcare references.

JOE

I saw Serena in the incubator shortly after she was born. She was asleep. She had become pink. She had a good dozen or more wires for monitoring plus an IV for calories attached to her. And she weighed less than five pounds. I looked at her closely and I noticed that she had my hands and feet. I thought, "Egads. This strange creature who looks like ET or something is in fact a Palau." That was when I realized the total identification I had with her.

JANET

My first feelings after birth hardly reflected great maternal instinct. I remember my doctor putting Jack on my belly just after he was born. "It's a boy," she said, and I thought, "All this for a boy?" Then Tyler was beside me crying. He was so moved. They put Jack in a little blanket and handed him to Tyler. There was Tyler holding Jack and crying and I thought, "This is it? I'm glad Tyler and Jack like each other, I mean, but I don't feel anything." My two main thoughts on the delivery table were how awful the pain was and how I lacked any maternal instinct. But then they brought Jack to me in recovery and I was able to hold him and really look at him. I was so moved. It was marvelous.

HELEN

I had a difficult first birth experience for a number of reasons. I was prepared and anxious to deliver vaginally, however I also was warned by my physician that my history of herpes might affect my ability to do so. If any sign of a herpes outbreak was seen, I'd automatically be scheduled for a Cesarean section because of the risk of infection to the baby. However, it wasn't until I already was in labor, having contractions three minutes apart with a bad case of the shakes, that my doctor found a little pimple on my genitals. For the next three hours, she poked and probed this pimple trying to figure out whether or not it was something to be concerned about, and in the end decided that she couldn't be sure it was harmless. Suddenly, I was scheduled for a C-section.

I have to say that I wasn't fighting the decision at that point. I'd been having strong contractions every three minutes and was progressing slowly nonetheless. After six hours I had dilated only two centimeters.

I was scheduled to have an epidural, and I remember that they had some kind of problem and tried to administer it three times. The first time I remember that they drew blood, the second time some kind of fluid, and the last time they finally got the anesthesia to work.

I just remember being so scared and upset that I was totally uninvolved with the birth. I had a funny feeling in my nose and my shoulder. I kept on asking how my vital signs were. And when they delivered the baby, I just wasn't really concerned with her. I was just thinking about myself. I really felt as if something was wrong with me. I remember one moment when they lifted her up so that I could see her that I started to cry because I was so happy, but then they whisked her away to the nursery because she had a slight breathing problem. And from that point on, it was just hysteria.

I got some sort of tranquilizer or sedative right after the surgery, but I still remember being in terrible pain when I was moved from the operating table to the bed. It turned out that the anesthesiologist had punctured the sheath around my spinal cord during the epidural procedure and I was leaking spinal fluid. So the first hours and even days after my birth were spent flat on my back in really awful pain while the doctors tried to figure out what the problem was and how to remedy it. I would see my daughter and try to hold her, but I was in so much discomfort that I couldn't really get into mothering. Her father was the one who really was able to comfort her.

PART 1
THE FIRST DAYS

1

AFTER BIRTH

All of us have seen the photographs of new mothers at the end of our pregnancy manuals. Their beatific expressions glow with pride and love for the newborn in their arms. Usually in bold type next to the picture is a quote from the mother about her feelings of triumph, strength, and elation after having delivered her healthy child into the world. Can you expect to have that sense of triumph and elation after you deliver?

You certainly can hope for such a happy outcome, but expecting that you'll feel a certain way about yourself and your newborn right after birth can lead to disappointment. A woman's first reactions to motherhood will be shaped by her pregnancy, labor, and delivery, as well as by her feelings about motherhood. Each woman's first moments as a mother will be unique.

How you feel after the birth of your child will depend not only on your baby's condition, but on yours as well. The mother whose labor and delivery were short and uncomplicated will undoubtedly feel stronger and perhaps more convivial than the woman who labored for thirty hours before having an emergency Cesarean section.

Some women do walk off the table and phone their mothers with the news. Many more, however, are satisfied to rest in bed admiring their child and spending some quiet time with their partners. Though tired, they're too excited to go to sleep. And the lasting effects of the local or other anesthetics used during the birth stave off any postpartum discomfort for a couple of hours, making this the perfect time to become acquainted with the new member of the family.

Women who have particularly difficult births, however, may want to be left in the quiet of their room to sleep and collect themselves. Sometimes they may not even want to spend much time with the baby, so strong is the urge to have some peaceful time alone. New mothers who yearn for this rest period and who are not overwhelmed immediately by their maternal feelings often feel guilty about their desire to be alone or just with their partners for a little while. But these feelings fall into the normal range. There's nothing wrong with a woman, exhausted and at her limit following her birth, wanting a few quiet hours to recuperate from the trauma.

Helen's and Marie's stories are good examples of how your unique birth experience will determine what you're going to feel just after your baby is born. However, even though there's no way to foretell exactly what your postpartum condition will be, you can be acquainted with some of the more common postpartum procedures and reactions so that you won't be surprised or frightened if you feel them:

DISCOMFORT DURING STITCHING

With a final, tired effort, you deliver the placenta after your baby is born. From what your childbirth books say, your work is finally over and you can relax with your partner and new baby. But your doctor or midwife tells you that there's one more procedure to go, repairing an epiosotomy and/or any vaginal tears that occurred during the birth.

The episiotomy is an incision made in the perineum—the tissue between the anus and the vagina—to prevent the baby from tearing the tissue during birth. Not every woman needs an epiosotomy. Some women's perineums, if stretched and massaged during delivery, can accommodate the delivery of the head without tearing. Episiotomies are fairly routine today, however. If you want your doctor or midwife to try stretching and massaging the perineum area before performing an episiotomy, make sure you make that arrangement with him or her before your delivery.

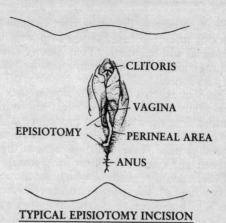

CLITORIS

VAGINA

EPISIOTOMY

PERINEAL AREA

ANUS

TYPICAL EPISIOTOMY INCISION

Some deliveries result in tearing of the perineum and/or the vagina. These tears require stitching much as an episiotomy does.

If you have a regional anesthetic, like an epidural, or extensive local anesthesia, like a pudendal block, the episiotomy repair will probably be performed while the anesthetic is still in effect. If you have had no pain medication, a local anesthetic probably will be injected into the perineum to numb the area for suturing. Even with this injection, however, you may find the episiotomy repair uncomfortable. It might seem odd that after coping with the pain of labor and delivery without wanting medication, you can't sit still for five minutes of stitching. However, consider your mental as well as your physical state. You have used intense control over yourself to manage the pain of labor and then used all of your strength to deliver your baby. At this point any discomfort may seem like too much to bear.

Even if you feel that insult is being added to injury, however, it's important to relax and lie quietly. Obviously, the stitching will go more quickly. Secondly, if your muscles are tight in the area being repaired, the stitches may be too tight once the normal swelling of the healing tissue occurs the following day. Tight stitches pull on the irritated area and make the incision more uncomfortable than necessary. Try using your Lamaze breathing techniques or just deep breathing to help you relax your vaginal muscles and lie quietly. Your partner can help you by breathing along with you and reminding you to keep your muscles loose.

The kind of stitches that your doctor uses to repair your episiotomy may have some effect on your postpartum comfort. The most common procedure is the stitch-and-knot method whereby the physician ties off each suture above the skin line. These can press against the swollen, healing tissue and cause discomfort for a couple of weeks after delivery. Another method which accommodates the normal swelling of the perineal tissues is the running stitch, in which the suture is left unknotted so that the stitch can expand with the tissue. A third method involves closing the incision with stitches that never go completely through the skin. These also are reported to be more comfortable than the more common through-the-skin stitches favored by most doctors.

Through-the-skin stitches are the most common in part because they are the fastest and easiest stitches to use. And for some women this kind of repair causes no problem. However, if you would like your physician or midwife to use one of the other repair methods that may lessen postpartum discomfort, talk to him or her about that before your delivery.

Once your episiotomy has been repaired, your doctor may order an ice pack to place over the stitches during recovery rather than waiting until you are back in your room. The immediate use of ice packs is thought to prevent some of the normal swelling that occurs in the first days of healing. Once again, if you want to use ice packs to help ward off swelling of the perineum, make sure that you make the request to your doctor before you go into the hospital. Not all hospitals use ice packs as a preventive measure. Your doctor or midwife may have to make a special request to get them for you during recovery.

INVOLUTION

Involution refers to the process by which the uterus contracts and returns to its normal size. The whole involution process takes about six weeks.

Involution begins after the third stage of labor. When the placenta is delivered, the blood vessels feeding it are exposed and will continue to bleed. The initial stage of involution immediately after birth serves to compress these blood vessels in order to prevent hemorrhaging.

A nurse will knead and massage your uterus frequently to encourage the involution process. The massage usually is strong enough to be painful, but it is also brief. If you feel that your massage is unnecessarily rough, ask the nurse if she can be more gentle.

A nurse also will check the tone of your uterus from time to time after the birth to make sure that it is firm. If the uterus is not contracting as it should, you may be given an injection of oxytocin to encourage contractions and to prevent hemorrhaging.

The work being done by the uterus during the first hour or so after birth is remarkable. It begins with the full-term uterus whose top—the fundus—you could feel beneath your breastbone. In as little as half an hour after the birth, the uterus is the size of a 16-18 week pregnancy. Your nurse can help you feel how small the uterus has become in so short a time. The top now can be found between the navel and the pubic bone, and the uterus feels hard. It's about the size of a grapefruit.

INVOLUTION CRAMPS

The contractions of the involution process—especially if augmented by oxytocin—can be uncomfortable enough to make rest difficult. They often are described as intense menstrual cramps. If you're having trouble sleeping, your nurse may offer you some acetominophen (e.g., Tylenol) or acetominophen with codeine to relieve the pain.

SHAKING

Many women get the shivers just after giving birth. Their teeth chatter and their arms and legs shake uncontrollably for a few minutes to half an hour. If you know about these postpartum "shakes" you might even find them funny. However, if they're totally unexpected, the shivers can be frightening even though they're harmless.

The reason for the postpartum chills isn't entirely clear, although several causes have been suggested:
- They are a common aftereffect of epidural anesthesia.
- They often result from the tremendous physical exertion of labor and delivery.
- They may occur as a result of the normal loss of blood during delivery.
- The cool temperature of the delivery room might make you feel chilled if you're damp with sweat after the birth.

If you experience a postpartum chill, your doctor or attending nurse will probably offer you an extra blanket and a hot water bottle to help you warm up. You also can request that the room temperature be raised.

PINS AND NEEDLES

If you were given either a spinal or an epidural anesthetic, you'll probably feel pins and needles in your legs and feet as the drug wears off. The feeling is not unlike having the circulation return to a foot that has fallen asleep. The pins and needles sensation will probably start in the recovery room as the first signs of feeling when the anesthesia wears off. They start anywhere from a half hour to a couple of hours after delivery, depending on when your last dose of anesthesia was. You may find that the postpartum shakes aggravates the pins and needles, just as stepping on a sleeping foot increases that sensation. A couple of extra blankets might lessen your shivers, so ask for as many as make you comfortable.

HUNGER

Some new mothers can't think about food for a few hours after birth, but many find themselves ravenous. Probably you haven't eaten much since your labor started, yet you've worked strenuously for hours delivering your baby. Most Lamaze instructors will suggest that your partner have a sandwich on hand in case he gets hungry, but don't forget to pack one for yourself. Babies arrive at unusual hours, and you don't want to have to wait for the hospital kitchen to open to get something to eat.

TO NURSE OR NOT TO NURSE

In some hospitals you'll be asked while you're still in the delivery room whether or not you intend to nurse. If your answer is no, you may be given your first dose of milk suppressor right after delivery. This drug prevents milk production by inhibiting the production of prolactin— the hormone responsible for initiating lactation. The medication is supposed to prevent the painful engorgement that occurs in two or three days after milk production comes in. However, it is not always reliable, and some women become engorged despite taking a milk suppressor.

The delivery table is not the best place to make a decision about nursing or about taking a milk suppressor. You've been through a tremendous emotional and physical upheaval. Some women may have suffered enough during labor and delivery that the thought of any more physical work for the baby at that point is out of the question. On the other hand, some women who were sure that they didn't want to nurse now feel that they might want to reconsider after having met their new babies. You may want to wait until you've had some rest to make your final decision about nursing. Also, if you and your doctor haven't discussed the pros and cons of using hormone therapy versus the traditional breast binding method to stem milk production, you'll want some time to have that conversation before choosing hormone therapy. If an antilactogenic hormone (e.g., Parlodel) used to inhibit milk production is offered to you in the recovery room and you'd like some time to consider whether or not you want to take the medication, ask your midwife or doctor to postpone treatment for a few hours.

If you know that you want to nurse, on the other hand, you might want to put the baby to your breast during the time you have together immediately after delivery. Your baby's response will depend on several factors, including natural ability, the baby's condition, and the kind of medications used during the delivery. Some newborns suckle effortlessly when they are just born, but others need some encouragement during the first few days to get the hang of it. Keep in mind that if you've had any sedatives or tranquilizers during the course of your labor, your baby will be groggy from those drugs right after birth. After a good sleep, he or she will probably nurse with more vigor.

REST

Some new mothers are immediately overcome by exhaustion after birth. After a quick look at the baby and a hug for their partners, they welcome the quiet of their hospital room and the few hours of sleep they can get before the first feeding. Some of us, however, are so excited after birth that we don't notice how tired we are. Even if you didn't lose any sleep the night before your birth, you've still been through a physically exhausting ordeal. Don't let your elation fool you into thinking that you don't need a rest. While your baby is sleeping after his or her difficult entrance into the world, you should be too.

FOR CESAREAN BIRTHS

For most first-time mothers, having a Cesarean birth is an emotional and physical trial. Often, Cesarean deliveries follow an attempt at vaginal delivery, so the new mother has already gone through several hours of unproductive labor and is worn out by the time a Cesarean section is recommended.

Fortunately, more liberal attitudes and advances in anesthesiology offer parents-to-be several options that can minimize the trauma of the Cesarean operation. The mother often can choose a regional anesthetic so that she can be awake during and after the delivery much as she would be during and after a vaginal birth. Also, in many hospitals, her partner is allowed to be with her and offer support during the operation and recovery.

If the mother does have a regional anesthetic, she and her partner will be able to share the first moments after birth becoming acquainted with the new member of the family. Her partner will be able to hold the baby and prop him or her up so that Mom can get a good look at her new creation while she's having her incision repaired.

For many women, being with their newborns and partners during and after a Cesarean section makes an otherwise difficult birth joyous. Given the high rate of Cesarean births (up to 25 percent in some hospitals), it would be wise to ask your doctor how surgical deliveries are handled in your hospital so that you can request options such as regional anesthesia or presence of a partner should the need for Cesarean delivery arise.

The condition of the mother after a Cesarean birth is as individual as that of the mother who had a vaginal delivery. Much will depend on the length of the labor before the C-section and the kind of anesthesia administered. The sensations a mother may experience after the delivery of her child include the following:

DISCOMFORT DURING REPAIR

After the baby is delivered, the surgeon will remove the placenta and examine it to make sure that it is whole and no tissue remains in the uterus. The next step is to repair the incision in the uterus and allow the intestines and bladder to return to their normal positions. Then the obstetrician will begin repairing the layers of abdominal tissues that were cut by the incision. As many as five or six layers of stitches may be needed to close the incision, so the process can take some time—forty-five minutes or more.

Some women who have regional anesthesia can *feel* the repair process following the delivery of the baby. They don't actually feel pain, which is blocked by the anesthetic, but they feel the pulling and pushing as the tissues and organs are manipulated during and after delivery. Tell your doctor if you're in discomfort and then try using your childbirth breathing techniques to help you relax and cope with the discomfort.

Incision Placement. Many new mothers think of their incisions as one deep cut through the skin and into the uterus. Actually, two separate incisions are made—one through the skin and another through the uterine wall. The placement of these incisions may or may not mirror each other.

Essentially, there are four types of incisions: the transverse or (Pfannestiel) skin incision which runs horizontally close to the pubic bone (colloquially known as the *bikini* incision); the vertical skin incision running from navel to pubic bone; the lower segment uterine incision running horizontally through the lower portion of the uterus; and the classical or vertical uterine incision which cuts longitudinally through the uterus from the navel to pubic bone. These four kinds of incisions will be combined to perform the safest possible surgical delivery for both the baby and the mother. A mother may have a transverse skin incision and a classical uterine incision, for instance, or vice versa. However, transverse skin and lower segment uterine incisions are preferred for the following reasons, and are used routinely today unless an emergency demands the faster classical incision be performed:

•The lower segment uterine incision goes through fewer muscles and repairs faster and stronger than the classical incision making vaginal birth in the future a possibility.

•Lower segment abdominal incisions are more desirable cosmetically because they leave only a small, low scar that would be covered by bikini pants.

If you know in advance that you'll be having a Cesarean section, you might want to tell your doctor that you

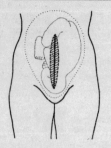

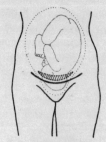

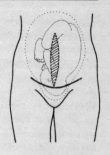

VERTICAL SKIN/CLASSICAL UTERINE INCISION	TRANSVERSE SKIN/LOWER SEGMENT UTERINE INCISIONS	TRANSVERSE SKIN/CLASSICAL UTERINE INCISIONS

have a preference for the lower segment incisions. You might also request that the outer incision be lower segment even if the inner uterine incision has to be classic. The deciding factor in where the incision is placed, however, will be the course of your birth.

EFFECTS OF ANESTHESIA

If you have a Cesarean, you'll be given one of three types of anesthesia: spinal, which goes into the spinal fluid and effects a regional block; epidural, which is administered in the space around the spinal cord and also effects a regional block; or general. The kind of anesthesia given depends on what condition you and your baby are in and what kind of experience the anesthesiologist has had. Thus, it would be to your advantage to talk to your doctor or midwife about the anesthesiologists on staff at the hospital or maternity center where you're delivering. You may want to specify a particular anesthesiologist trained in a form of anesthesia attractive to you. In an emergency, your choice may be overridden; however, if time allows, your request should be honored.

If there's an emergency and every minute counts until the baby is delivered, you'll probably be given a general anesthesia. A general anesthetic becomes effective almost immediately and allows the baby to be delivered in minutes.

If time allows, however, you'll more likely be given a spinal or epidural anesthetic. These can take up to twenty minutes to become effective. The epidural is considered the most sophisticated regional anesthetic and takes skill and experience to introduce. If there is no anesthesiologist available who has experience with epidurals, a spinal anesthetic most often will be administered.

If you have a spinal or epidural, you'll be awake during and after your surgery. You may also have been given a tranquilizer, however, which will make you groggy. After the surgery, you'll probably benefit from the effects of the anesthetic for an hour or two more, during which time you may want to stay with your partner and new baby. Whether or not your partner will be able to stay with you during surgery and after will depend on your doctor and your hospital's policies. Often standard policies are more conservative than what might be allowed if your doctor specifies an arrangement you've worked out before the delivery. However, without previous notification, the hospital staff is likely to stick rigidly to their policy regardless of your wishes. Make sure to ask beforehand that your partner be present during and after the birth if that is your desire.

The first sign that the anesthetic is wearing off probably will be the pins and needles feeling in your legs that is described above. When you start to feel this will depend on the kind of anesthetic used, when your last dose was given, and your individual response to the medication.

The period between the end of your surgery and the wearing off of the anesthesia may be a good time to give breastfeeding a try if you intend to nurse. You won't be feeling the involution contractions or any incision discomfort, so your first attempt will be comfortable and relaxed. Ask your nurse to suggest a position that you'll be able to use once the anesthesia wears off so that you can accustom yourself to it.

If you had spinal anesthesia you will be ordered to lie flat on your back for about twenty-four hours to prevent a headache that sometimes occurs after this type of anesthesia. However, with the help of your partner and a nurse, you too can put the newborn to the breast for the first time.

As mentioned above, don't be surprised if your baby isn't interested. Because of the medications given to you or just the baby's need for some encouragement, breast-feeding might take some time to become *natural* for the new baby and the new mother.

The picture for mothers who have general anesthesia during a Cesarean is often quite different. You may be groggy during the half hour or so after the operation, when the anesthesia is wearing off. Your throat might also be sore from being intubated, that is, from having a tube placed in your mouth and throat during surgery to prevent any liquid or vomit from being introduced into the lungs. Nausea and vomiting also are fairly common after-effects of general anesthesia.

When you become more alert, you may already be uncomfortable from the involution cramps and the incision, and may require an injection of a pain reliever, which will once again make you groggy.

Obviously, the early recovery from a surgical birth is a difficult period. Your partner can help out by reassuring you and telling you about the new member of the family. If the baby is in good condition, you might want to see him or her and have the baby placed in your arms for a few minutes before you go to sleep.

RECOVERY ROOM PROTOCOL

In the recovery room you'll probably be roused frequently by the hospital staff checking your blood pressure and temperature, assisting you in simple leg exercises to prevent blood clots from forming, and asking you to breathe deeply to prevent the collection of any mucus in the lungs and postoperative pneumonia. All of this attention is not meant to annoy you but to ascertain that you are recovering without complications. When the effects of the anesthesia used during the surgery have worn off enough for your nurse to make sure that you've suffered no ill effects from the medication or from the surgery, you'll be removed from the recovery room and brought to your room on the postpartum floor. Your baby will be brought to the nursery and you'll both have a chance to get some rest.

DEEP BREATHING   This simple exercise prevents post-operative lung congestion caused by collection of mucus and fluid in the lungs during surgery under anesthesia. It does double duty, however, as a gentle abdominal exercise that stimulates the bowel through mild tightening and relaxing of the abdominal muscles and aids the passage of gas that often collects in the bowel after surgery.

Lie comfortably on your back. Place your hands on your abdomen. Slowly take a breath in through your nose. Think about filling a cavity from your hands up to your throat with the breath. First take the air as far down as you can into your abdomen, expanding it with the breath. Then fill your diaphragm and finally your upper chest. When you've inhaled as deeply as you can, let out the air slowly from your mouth. Exhale as thoroughly as possible, tightening the abdominal muscles to push out the last bit of air. Repeat three to five times an hour.

LEG EXERCISES   One simple exercise, the "Leg Brace," calls for tightening the muscles in your calves, thighs, and buttocks, holding for a moment and then

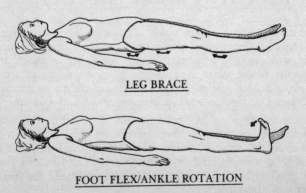

LEG BRACE

FOOT FLEX/ANKLE ROTATION

relaxing. The exercise is repeated three to five times. The tensing and relaxing of the muscles encourages circulation in the legs.

Another easy exercise that encourages blood flow in the legs is "Foot Flexing/Ankle Rotation." First, flex one foot, then extend it. Repeat three to five times and then do the same with the other foot. Following this stretch, rotate each foot first in clockwise and then counterclockwise circles. Repeat three to five times.

FEVER

A low-grade temperature of 100°F or less is fairly common after a surgical delivery. However, a fever that is higher than 100°F often indicates an infection that will require treatment. The nursing staff in the recovery room and on the postpartum floor will keep a close watch on your temperature to make sure that it remains in the normal range.

INVOLUTION CRAMPS AFTER CESAREAN

Mothers who deliver by Cesarean have the same uterine involution as mothers who deliver vaginally. Often the post-Cesarean mother will be given some oxytocin to encourage uterine contractions and enhance the involution process. The oxytocin will make the involution cramps stronger and more uncomfortable. Aside from the painkillers you will be given, you may want to use the breathing you were taught in childbirth classes to help cope with the discomfort. Post-Cesarean mothers also will have their abdomen massaged to speed uterine involution. Because of the raw incision, the massage can be quite painful for the couple of seconds it lasts. However, it does only last a couple of seconds, and that reassurance in addition to the use of your labor breathing techniques can make the process more bearable.

PAIN RELIEF

After the anesthetic used during the Cesarean section wears off, most women begin to feel discomfort at the incision, and require some fairly strong pain medication in the first twenty-four hours to allow them to rest adequately. You're better off not waiting until the pain is unbearable before asking for pain relief. Enduring unbearable pain during or after childbirth is no sign of courage or womanhood, rather it takes away from what can be an extraordinary and thrilling event that happens only once or twice in most women's lives.

When you start to feel discomfort, tell your nurse and she'll administer a painkiller (e.g., meperidine [Demerol] or morphine) by injection. If you're nursing, you'll be given a medication that won't have adverse effects on your baby, but ask the nurse administering the medication for reassurance about your ability to nurse just to ease your mind.

Whether you deliver vaginally or by Cesarean section, after your postpartum sleep you'll wake up to the rigors and joys of feeding, holding, and caring for your newborn. You'll also wake up to the aches and pains of your body, which is starting to recover from the trauma of the birth. The more you know about what feelings to expect when you wake up, the better you'll be able to cope with and enjoy your first days as a mother.

STEVE

I remember that the maternity floor staff seemed to lack any consensus on what were important issues to Marie and myself during our three days there. Every nurse had different advice about breastfeeding, leaving lights on at night, and even showing the baby to visitors. The breastfeeding issue was particularly important since I felt Marie's success at nursing was really the first acid test of our ability as parents. If we couldn't feed Willie, how could we take him home?

MARIE

The first half day in the hospital, I had a typical arrangement whereby the baby was brought to me for feedings every four hours and then whisked back to the nursery. I was lonely for my son during the intervening hours, though, and was fortunate to have the option of rooming-in, which I took. Willie was with me all day and night except during visiting hours when he was taken to the nursery. I found these first few days of closeness invaluable. During the hours I had to absorb myself in the wonderful tiny details of my new baby, the discomfort from the repaired tears in my vagina and perineum was muted. I was able to nurse Willie on demand instead of on the hospital's schedule, and could practice diapering, cleaning his umbilical cord and comforting him at the hospital when expert help was nearby. What Steve said is true. It seemed that everyone had a different opinion, which was irritating at times, but having Willie with me around the clock gave me many opportunities to try different methods of handling him until I came upon the one that suited us both.

LAURIE

I had these horrible hemorrhoids as well as an episiotomy incision. I couldn't even find a sitting position for nursing that was comfortable. The ice packs that the staff constantly changed were a great help, but I really thank God for the topical anesthetic spray. I don't know what I would have done without that stuff. I still have some left over because I bought so much of it when I came home.

I know that there are women who have sex right after they deliver, but I was absolutely horrified at the suggestion. When my doctor came in and told me that I'd have to wait at least four weeks before I could have sex, I looked at him stupified. I wanted to say, "Sex! Are you crazy?"

2

THE FIRST THREE DAYS

Your new role as a mother begins as soon as you leave the recovery room. Because of your own tiredness, soreness, and hormonal changes, you may be surprised by your lack of tolerance for any stress. The most self-composed woman who worked right up until she delivered might find herself dissolving in tears when the food isn't appealing or the baby won't nurse on the first try. She also might feel so incapacitated that she doubts her ability to take care of her child once she leaves the hospital. She may even be angry when she is woken up for the night feedings that she requested—and then feel guilty about her anger.

All these fears and conflicting feelings are normal—especially on the first day. Often, it's hard to find the time to sort them out in the hospital because of the scheduled visits of doctors and nurses as well as the entourage of unscheduled visitors—friends and relatives who decide to come by even though you strongly suggested that they wait a few days to give you time to rest. (For some reason the notion persists that a new mother needs company at the hospital to lift her spirits despite the most earnest request for some peace and quiet.)

A lot of the tumult of feelings you have will be resolved as you fall into a comfortable routine of mothering and as hormonal stability is regained. However, some of the anxieties of this first day can be avoided altogether by knowing what to expect when you wake up after giving birth. If you are familiar with common postpartum symptoms, you won't be scared if you're dizzy, have a raw, sore episiotomy incision, or a maddening, dull ache at the bottom of your back. Also, you'll know what you can do to make yourself feel more comfortable. Sometimes taking control of some part of an unfamiliar situation can help you feel less anxious about the rest of it.

The following are common postpartum symptoms. Some women experience all of them, some few. Some feel them very intensely while others barely notice them. It all depends on what your delivery was like and how you react to the physiological and psychological aftereffects of childbirth. Bear in mind that your reaction will be in keeping with your individual makeup and therefore can't be judged as better or worse than another woman's postpartum response. Your postpartum course will be as individual and unique as your pregnancy.

POSTPARTUM BLEEDING

Accompanying the involution process that restores the uterus to its original size is the lochia, a bloody discharge similar to a menstrual period, though longer lasting and heavier. After birth, the body must rid itself of uterine lining tissue and of blood from the vessels at the site of placental attachment that are being sealed off by involution. In the first day, the flow may be quite heavy and bright red. It will continue to be red for a few days and then will begin to darken.

You'll be given large sanitary napkins with a belt to absorb the discharge. If your episiotomy is painful, you might find that pressing the pad against the stitches is too uncomfortable. In that case, you might want to buy self-adhesive pads that attach to your panties. The fit against you will be looser, so the chance of an accident will be greater. However, you'll probably be far more comfortable.

Your nurse also will keep an absorbent pad under you on the bed to catch any leakage. The pad should be changed frequently.

The use of tampons to absorb the discharge is discouraged because inserting anything into the vagina increases the chance of introducing bacteria, which then could migrate through the still open cervix into the uterus and cause an infection.

When you first get out of bed, you may feel a warm gush of blood empty from your vagina. Some new mothers are frightened by this sudden flow and think that they're starting to hemorrhage. Most often, however, the gush is simply lochia that has collected in the vagina while you were reclining. Upon arising, the pooled discharge flows out all at once.

Contractions caused by nursing (see "Nursing Cramps," p. 31) also will increase the flow, so be sure to change your sanitary pad before you start to feed your baby to prevent leaking.

The discharge is not irritating or painful in any way. However, it can frighten a new mother if she's uninformed and sees this substantial flow of blood following her birth. All of us have been warned, after all, that a bright red discharge is cause for alarm. If for any reason you feel concerned that you are bleeding too much, don't hesitate to ask your doctor or nurse to examine you. If your lochia is abnormally heavy, your doctor might want to look into the cause of the heavy flow. Even if you're within the normal range, a check for good measure will help reassure you that your recovery is coming along fine.

The lochia usually lasts four to six weeks in all, with the discharge going from red to brownish red to yellow in the final days. Some clots may be passed, especially after you've been lying down, since the blood may pool in the vagina and then be passed in clotted form. Clots of even a couple of inches in diameter shouldn't concern you if they are not accompanied by an increase in blood flow and change in color of the discharge to bright red again.

> Clots accompanied by a heavy, bright red blood flow are not normal and should be brought to the attention of your doctor or midwife.

Some women notice a strong meaty odor accompanying the discharge, especially in the first couple of weeks. The odor is probably caused by the dead tissue being sluffed off the uterus along with the blood and is a normal part of the healing process.

YOUR BREASTS

After you deliver the placenta, prolactin, the hormone that initiates the production of milk in your breasts, is released into your system. You won't be producing any true milk in the first two or three days. Instead, a thick, yellowish fluid called colostrum or early milk will be secreted. Nursing mothers feel that their babies aren't being nourished enough by the colostrum during the days before milk production starts, but colostrum actually is a substance much like breast milk. It contains less sugar and fat but more of a certain kind of protein and is very nutritious for the newborn.

ENGORGEMENT

When your breasts do begin producing true milk, the blood supply to the alveoli will increase dramatically. In just a few hours—often while you're napping—the increase in circulation and collection of milk will swell the milk-producing glands, making the breasts rock hard, lumpy, hot, and painful. The feeling is not unlike the feverish breasts you might have experienced during early pregnancy, only the sensation is greatly exaggerated. Though you've probably heard and read about engorgement, you're still likely to be surprised by the size, hardness, and feverishness of your breasts.

If you're nursing, a good way to relieve this painful engorgement is to nurse your baby and/or pump some of the fluid from your breasts often. Bottlefeeding mothers will be helped somewhat by milk suppression procedures.

MILK SUPPRESSION

Women who are bottlefeeding will want to suppress milk production. They can accomplish this by binding their breasts or by taking a milk suppressor. Breast-binding has been used for generations to stem milk production by pressure and lack of stimulation. The new mother wears a tight bra after birth. When the breasts become engorged, she applies ice packs to them, which decrease metabolism and the rate of milk formation. The painful engorgement lasts about a day, though some discomfort may persist for two or three more days. Acetominophen (e.g., Tylenol) is prescribed to ease the discomfort during the two or three days of engorgement. Also, expressing a small amount of colostrum may reduce the discomfort of engorgement without stimulating milk production enough to reduce the effectiveness of the binding procedure.

The alternative to binding is to use a milk suppressor called Parlodel. Parlodel prohibits the release of the hormone prolactin, which is responsible for initiating lactation. By interrupting milk production, Parlodel is supposed to prevent the uncomfortable engorgement of the breasts that occurs in the first week after birth. The normal treatment calls for the drug to be taken orally for fourteen days.

Many women turn to a milk suppressor because they are anxious about being painfully engorged for several days. However, it's important for the new mother to realize that this medication, like any other, has side effects and variable effectiveness. For one woman, engorgement is completely prevented; for another some tenderness occurs regardless of the drug therapy. Some women experience dizziness during treatment caused by slightly lowered blood pressure. Another common occurrence is rebounding after the medication is stopped, when the breasts become tender and swollen for a day or two following treatment.

Of course for some new mothers the benefits of using a milk suppressor will outweigh the risks. But as with any part of the birth experience, it's wise to talk over the risks and benefits of taking Parlodel with your doctor before you deliver your baby so that you have time to weigh the pros and cons and make an unhurried decision about how you want to inhibit milk production.

If after starting the hormone therapy you decide that you want to give nursing a try, don't feel that you've lost that option. Ask your doctor if you can stop the treatment and encourage milk production. In many instances, the early effects of the milk suppressor can be reversed and the new mother can nurse successfully.

EARLY NURSING

Nursing is one of a mother's earliest and most satisfying means of communicating with her newborn. Once mother and baby have worked out a system comfortably for both of them, these fifteen or twenty minute interludes provide precious intimate moments when the baby can explore his or her mother's face and come to recognize her smell and voice, and when Mom can linger over each detail of her new baby and delight in each new movement and facial expression.

Keep in mind, however, that breastfeeding may not come naturally to you or your baby. Sometimes a baby needs some encouragement to suck properly and to hold the nipple in the mouth the right way. The baby's mouth should cover the whole nipple and most of the aureola to stimulate milk production and the letdown reflex properly. This may seem like an awesome mouthful for a tiny infant, and many new mothers make the mistake of allowing the newborn to suck on the nipple only. This doesn't stimulate the breast properly and can lead to increased nipple soreness. Remember, also, to nurse only for a few minutes on each side during the first few days to prevent nipple soreness. Five minutes on a side is sufficient.

Learning to nurse with confidence takes time and practice. Information and support can make your initiation into breastfeeding much easier and more satisfying. Check with your obstetrician for parent education programs in your area that provide nursing instruction for mothers-to-be and new mothers. Another good source of information is *The Complete Book of Breastfeeding* by Marvin S. Eiger, M.D., and Sally Wendkos Olds (Bantam, 1987). Keep the book on hand as a reference when you're in the hospital.

You might also want to contact your local La Leche League's chapter for experienced advice. The La Leche League's sole purpose is to support and inform breastfeeding mothers. If you can't find a listing in your local phone book, contact La Leche League International, 9616 Minneapolis Avenue, Franklin Park, Illinois 60131, for information about a chapter in your area. One caveat about this group is that the members tend to be *avid* supporters of on-demand, around-the-clock nursing. Their orthodox doctrines put off some mothers with more flexible nursing arrangements. You don't have to accept the total La Leche philosophy to benefit from this network of support groups for nursing mothers, however.

If you are depending solely on the nursing staff at your hospital to help you learn a nursing technique that is comfortable for you and your baby, make sure to inquire whether special staff is provided for this purpose. Some hospitals have lactation consultants who provide excellent advice and support. In others, however, you may see a number of different nurses, all of whom have different ideas about the best way to nurse. And the attending nursing staff may be too busy to give you the individual attention you need to get your breastfeeding off to a good start.

If you find that your hospital doesn't have specialized programs to assist breastfeeding mothers, ask your obstetrician or midwife if any other local parent education programs offer lactation consultations.

MILK SUPPLY IN MOTHERS SEPARATED FROM THEIR INFANTS

Most new mothers start to nurse with their newborns at the breast in the hospital bed. However, a wide range of complications can separate mother and infant for the first few days or even the first week or two.

If you have a baby who needs to be in the intensive care nursery after birth, or if you develop some kind of postpartum infection, you may not be able to nurse your newborn as you'd like. However, there's no reason to give up on breastfeeding altogether. New mothers who use a breast pump can get an adequate milk supply started while separated from their infants and at the same time provide their newborns with the benefits of mother's milk. Though a manual pump may be adequate, an electric pump is probably the most satisfactory solution for the recuperating mother. In the hospital, you'll probably be offered one. If you need to use an electric pump at home, make sure to ask someone on the hospital staff before you're discharged where you might rent one. Another source of information is your local La Leche League chapter. If they don't have a pump to lend you, they'll know where you can get one.

Your pediatrician will give you instructions for using the pump. Usually you'll use it every three to four hours, day and night. If you can, store the milk and bring it in to feed your newborn. Though not as direct, you'll get the satisfaction of nursing your baby and will feel rewarded for getting up to feed the "iron baby" in the middle of the night.

FOR BOTTLEFEEDING MOTHERS

There is a fashionable way to do everything, and that extends to the way we give birth to and feed our children as well. It wasn't long ago that opinion leaned toward heavily sedating the mother during birth and bottlefeeding the baby with formula on a strict schedule. Now "natural" childbirth is in vogue, as is breastfeeding on demand. The pendulum has swung hard in the other direction, and for new mothers who are truly uncomfortable with breastfeeding—or for those who are unable to nurse because they are returning to work immediately, have had previous breast surgery, or have breast abnormalities that make nursing impossible—peer pressure can make the decision to bottlefeed a difficult one. It is true that most medical professionals consider breast milk the optimum food for the newborn's first six months of life. However, of equal importance in our society, where sanitary conditions, clean water, and an adequate supply of formula are readily available, is the emotional satisfaction of the feeding sessions.

A majority of the time you spend with your newborn in the first few weeks will be during feedings. These are the times when you'll stop whatever else you're doing and take the time to hold, rock, and talk to your baby. Chances are that if you're anxious and uncomfortable giving the breast to your baby, feedings will be a battleground rather than a satisfying interaction. Your baby, picking up on your tension, will become nervous and fussy too, prolonging the nursing session that you'd just as soon get over. The more anxious you become, the harder it is to relax enough for the let-down reflex to occur. Then the baby gets more anxious because he's hungry and getting no milk, which makes you more anxious, and so the cycle continues.

If your experience with breastfeeding is not a good one, talk to your pediatrician. He or she may offer some suggestions that make nursing more enjoyable. However, if you simply can't stand the notion of breastfeeding (or if you can't nurse), you'll be doing yourself and your baby a favor by bottlefeeding without guilt. Your baby needs the emotional nourishment of these feeding sessions as much as the nutritional nourishment. He or she needs to feel loved and secure in this strange new environment, and you need the emotional nourishment that comes from satisfying your baby's needs and deepening your attachment to him or her.

NURSING CRAMPS

Nursing mothers may notice that whenever they breastfeed in the first few days the contractions of the involuting uterus intensify to the point of pain. These cramps are caused by the release of oxytocin prompted by the baby's sucking, and they speed the involution process. Oxytocin is responsible not only for the let-down reflex that allows the milk to flow from the nipple but also for contractions of the uterus which encourage the involution process. If your cramps are particularly intense, help yourself through them by making sure that you are in a comfortable position, taking a deep breath when you start to breastfeed, and then using your labor breathing techniques to help you stay relaxed until the cramping subsides.

STITCHES

Stitches used to repair vaginal tears or an episiotomy—the incision made in the perineum tissue between the rectum and the vagina during delivery—may feel sore though not uncomfortable when you're lying down. However, when you sit up, get out of bed or walk, the stitches may throb and ache as if they were coming apart. You may worry that if you take another step, all of the stitches will tear. But there's really no reason for that kind of concern. Stitches are very strong and will tear only if greatly strained.

What you're most likely feeling is the pull of the stitches against the swollen perineal tissue. The perineum and vagina respond to injury as would any other part of the body and will become swollen and tender as a result of the bruising, tearing, or episiotomy made during the birth.

Unlike other parts of the body, however, the tissues in this area are delicate and sensitive. Furthermore, we can't see the injury in order to put it in proper perspective. Think of how a canker sore feels on your tongue, for instance. Judging from how it feels in your mouth, you'd think that it was a large sore, but when you look in the mirror you see that it's just a small white bump. Somehow, seeing how small the sore is makes the discomfort less disturbing. Your stitches are similar in that they feel as if you've been disfigured, judging by the sensation of the painful lump between your legs. Your nurse and doctor, however, can see that you really look quite normal, albeit swollen. Ask the person examining you if you can look at yourself with the help of a mirror. Just seeing how normal the area looks can assuage the fears that you've been permanently injured during delivery.

Such reassurances can make you feel less anxious, but they probably won't eliminate the discomfort of your stitches. For relief, most new mothers are offered an analgesic such as Tylenol and a local anesthetic spray. Don't be shy about accepting these comforting measures. The pain medication given to you won't affect your ability to nurse. In fact, it may make it easier for you to care for your baby. Newborns often can sense and be upset by tension in their mothers. Pain makes you tense, so relieving your pain is something you can do for you and your new baby.

Your nurse also will suggest applying ice packs to the stitches, as well as exposing them to light for a few minutes several times a day. Another soothing measure is the sitz bath, which can help reduce swelling and promote healing.

A sitz bath is simply a soak in hot water. You'll probably be given a pan that fits inside the toilet seat in your room. You fill the pan with hot water and soak the stitches for ten to twenty minutes. The notion of sitting anywhere may seem impossible, but these soaks, done several times a day, really soothe the area and relieve discomfort.

The problem with the sitz bath isn't that it's too painful to sit down and soak, it's finding the time three times a day to get into the bathroom for twenty minutes. Between feedings, visits from the obstetrician and pediatrician, meals, and hospital visiting hours, many new mothers find that they only have time for a sitz bath once a night, when they're too tired to sit up for more than four or five minutes.

The remedy to this dilemma is to set aside a prescribed time every day for your soaks. But how are you supposed to work out your schedule with the nurses, the hospital mealtimes, and the doctors? Obviously, those interruptions are not easily controlled. The one part of your schedule you have control over is the visiting hours. Try to pare off twenty minutes on either side of the allotted time for your baths. One way to manage this is to send friends and relatives to the nursery with your partner to admire your beautiful baby before they visit with you.

Aside from measures to relieve your discomfort, your nurse will instruct you in the proper hygiene for your perineum while it heals. Most often, you'll be given a plastic bottle with a spray top (peri bottle) and a supply of antiseptic solution to cleanse the area thoroughly after going to the bathroom. Filling the bottle and rinsing yourself so thoroughly after every trip to the bathroom may seem bothersome, but it's an important part of reducing the risk of infection. You'll find also that the warm antiseptic rinse is soothing.

HEMORRHOIDS

Hemorrhoids are blood vessels (veins) near the anus that have become enlarged. In the case of pregnancy, the cause frequently is pressure on the veins from the enlarging uterus. Hemorrhoids often are irritated during pregnancy because many gravid women are constipated (see "Bowel Control," p. 37) and strain during their bowel movements. The straining puts further pressure on the hemorrhoids, irritating them and sometimes forcing a portion of them through the anus. During childbirth, the tremendous pressure of pushing the baby out aggravates any existing hemorrhoid condition and can sometimes cause one in a woman who didn't develop them all during her pregnancy.

Most new mothers who have hemorrhoids complain that they burn, itch, and are painful during a bowel movement or when sitting. Fortunately, most hemorrhoids connected with pregnancy and delivery disappear during recovery. However, while they are irritated, these swollen blood vessels can be extremely painful, and you'll want to use the various methods available to soothe them.

First, try tucking the portion of the blood vessel that has popped out of the anus back inside. Make sure the area is thoroughly cleansed and then use your fingers to press the tissue gently and carefully through the anus. The sitz bath so useful in relieving the pain of episiotomy stitches also helps soothe hemorrhoids as well. After a sitz bath, you may want to apply a Tucks pad (small gauze pad soaked in witch hazel) to the hemorrhoid to help keep swelling and irritation down. Anesthetic ointments as well as hemorrhoidal ointments also are available to control the burning and itching of these irritated tissues. Ask your nurse for one of these preparations if you feel that you need more relief.

Another important part of hemorrhoid care is to prevent any strain during bowel movements. Hard movements will cause you to strain and will irritate the hemorrhoids, so a stool softener will probably be prescribed for you. Some women are afraid that the stool softener, such as Colace, is like a laxative and will cause cramping and a forceful movement the following day. However, these stool softeners don't force a movement. Rather, they ensure that your natural urge to eliminate isn't discouraged by stool that is hard to pass.

SITTING AND STANDING

Getting out of bed can be a painful endeavor if you don't know how to save your lower back and perineum from the strain of movement. However, a few adjustments in maneuvering will help you avoid any discomfort.

First, remember to use your arms for leverage. Normally you use the muscles of your lower body to get up and sit down. But you want to take the strain off these muscles by using your arms to push you up when you want to stand or to lower you down when you want to sit.

Second, try to use the muscles of the vagina, rectum, and buttocks as a splint for the healing perineum. When you get up or sit down, tighten the muscles in this area

**USE ARMS TO PUSH OVER TO
AND UP FROM EDGE OF BED**

and hold them until you're in place. Then slowly release them. Some physicians suggest sitting on a pillow or rubber ring to save the stitches from the hard seat surface. Others suggest that using these devices only allows the perineum tissue to stretch more when you sit. They suggest that a hard surface actually supports the perineum better. You might want to try using a pillow or rubber ring, and then try sitting without cushioning on a chair. Whatever solution makes you most comfortable is the one you should use.

Third, ask your nurse for advice. If you try these techniques and still have a lot of pain moving around, ask a nurse to show you how to maneuver without discomfort.

Your first trip out of bed is likely to be the short walk to the bathroom. Most hospitals insist that you be accompanied by a nurse to the bathroom in case you feel faint or too weak. Remember that you've been lying down for several hours. Blood might be pooled in your legs, and when you stand suddenly you might feel dizzy or faint.

If you have an episiotomy you might also find that your incision begins to throb after you've been standing for a while. So even if you're feeling chipper and energetic when you're in bed, you might be faint and wobbly by the time you're halfway down the hall to the showers. You'll want a nurse there to reassure you and get you back into bed safely.

BOWEL CONTROL

Constipation is a fairly normal condition on the first couple of days after birth. First there is the hormonal factor. Progesterone, a hormone important in maintaining your pregnancy, is secreted in large amounts while you are pregnant. Progesterone also relaxes the smooth muscle in the body, which includes the bowel, so bowel activity frequently decreases during pregnancy, often causing constipation. After birth, the effect of progesterone lingers in the intestinal tract, causing continued bouts of constipation. Your normal bowel function may take a few weeks to reestablish itself.

Another factor is the flaccid condition of the abdominal muscles. Normally we use these to bear down and help evacuate the bowel. After birth, however, these muscles often are too weak to bear down effectively, so they can't help the slow-moving bowel as they did before.

The third factor is a psychological problem that complicates the physical ones. Many women who have stitches in the perineum or the vagina as well as those who developed hemorrhoids are afraid to have a bowel movement. They fear that the pressure exerted will cause more pain in that already sensitive area. This hesitancy might be translated into a suppression of the urge to have a bowel movement, which also aggravates a constipation problem.

Most often, new mothers will be given stool softeners after they deliver to make bowel movements easier and more comfortable. Drinking lots of liquids and eating fibrous fruits and vegetables also can help. Getting out of bed and moving around a little during the day is encouraged as well to help get your system going again.

When you do go to the bathroom, remember to use your hands to ease yourself down on the toilet, and try to hold in the muscles of the vagina and the buttocks. This will save the tissue around any stitches from stretching. You might even take a piece of tissue and apply counter-pressure to the episiotomy area to prevent pressure on the tissues. Then, try not to strain. A slight pressure assisting the natural contraction of the bowel should do the trick and not cause you much discomfort. When your bowel is empty, drop the tissue you used against your stitches directly into the toilet.

Careful cleansing of the area after a bowel movement is extremely important to avoid infecting the episiotomy repair and to prevent bacteria from being introduced into the vagina, where it might travel into the uterus and cause infection. Because of the sensitivity of the tissue near the anus, you might prefer washing with wet paper or a Tucks pad rather than wiping with dry. Remember to draw the paper from front to back and then drop it into the toilet. Then, flush the area with warm water from your peri bottle.

If by the second or third day you are uncomfortable because you have not been able to move your bowels, your physician might suggest a gentle laxative or a rectal suppository.

FLATULENCE

Some new mothers feel that they are full of intestinal gas and unable to prevent passing it. They don't seem to have the control over their rectal muscles that they normally do. The control will return as you recover, especially if you do the Kegel exercise (see p. 41) regularly. In the meantime, try to stay away from foods that tend to make you gassy, such as the cabbage family, dried beans, cucumbers, or any food to which you are particularly sensitive.

BLADDER CONTROL

As your uterus grew during pregnancy, it compressed your bladder, making you feel the need to urinate every other minute it seemed. Then, during labor, your bladder was pushed aside and your urethra stretched to allow for the baby to descend down the birth canal. During the birth itself, the bladder might have been bruised as the baby was forcefully pushed down the birth canal. Because of the rough treatment your bladder and urethra receive during pregnancy and childbirth, you may experience a variety of temporary problems with bladder control, including lack of sensation, inability to void, or leaking after a cough, laugh, or sneeze. The kind of problem you develop often reflects the course of your delivery, i.e., the use of anesthetics may lead to one kind of problem, the strain of delivering the baby vaginally another.

Regional anesthesia can lead to a lack of sensation in the pelvic region so that you don't feel the urge to void even when your bladder is full. If your bladder is bruised during birth, it also may lack sensitivity. In either case, the lack of feeling can be compounded by the loss of muscle tone in the abdomen, which can reduce awareness of a bloated bladder.

Because you may not sense your bladder becoming distended, your nurse will probably check to see if you've urinated or have had the urge to void a few hours after birth. If not, she might examine you to see if your bladder is full. Because stagnant urine is fertile ground for infection, your doctor may order catheterization in order to empty the bladder if you aren't feeling the need to void after a few hours. This simple procedure calls for a thin tube (the catheter) to be guided up the urethra and into the bladder so that urine can flow out through the tube into an attached receptacle. Catheterization can be uncomfortable, though the procedure usually takes only a few minutes. Relaxing the muscles in the area will make the procedure go a lot faster. Use your labor breathing to help you relax during catheterization.

A catheter also may be used if a new mother feels the need to void but can't pass any urine. This kind of blockage may be caused by the swelling around the urethra that may result from a vaginal delivery.

Leaking after a cough or a laugh may result from stretching of the urethra during birth and inadequate muscle support of the bladder and urethra after birth. In the postpartum woman, the pelvic floor muscles, which support the bladder and control urine flow, are flaccid. As a result, the angle of the bladder may change in such a way that any pressure on it, caused by coughing or laughing, for instance, would force urine down the urethra. The pelvic floor muscles, which tighten around the urethra to cut off the flow of urine are not strong enough to do so, and the urine leaks out.

For leaking as well as the other postpartum problems of bladder control, exercise to strengthen the pelvic floor muscles is the key to the return of normal function. The exercise recommended most often is the Kegel exercise (see p. 41). If you do this exercise faithfully, you've a good chance of regaining enough control to prevent leaking. Regaining control, however, will take time. Make sure that you practice good hygiene habits while the exercises are taking effect. Change your pad when you leak and cleanse the vulva and perineal area carefully with the antiseptic solution in your peri bottle. These steps will help to prevent irritation and possible infection.

Sensation in the bladder usually returns in the first day, and by the second the new mother may wish she couldn't feel the urge to urinate. Often by the time she's shuffled into the bathroom, urinated, cleaned up with the peri bottle, and shuffled back to bed, she feels as if she has to go again. These frequent bathroom trips reflect the body's effort to rid itself of the excess fluid retained during pregnancy.

EXERCISE

When your nurse comes in the day after you deliver and hands you a sheet with exercise instructions, you'll probably think she's crazy. The last thing you feel like doing is exercising. However, the regimen she'll show you is designed specifically for the postpartum woman to help speed her recovery. They improve circulation, strengthen lax supports to the bladder and uterus, and help prevent postural defects caused by weak abdominal muscles.

While the recommended exercises vary from hospital to hospital, the most common ones are variations on the following:

- Foot flexing or ankle rotation: (see illustration p. 18). These easy exercises encourage blood flow in the legs. First flex one foot, then extend it. Repeat three to five times, then do the same with the other foot. Next, rotate each foot first clockwise, then counterclockwise, three to five times.

- Kegel Exercise: Because this exercise is the underpinning of a successful recovery from childbirth, most of you were taught it during your childbirth classes and encouraged to perform it regularly throughout the day in the last few weeks of pregnancy as well as after birth. The Kegel exercise directly affects control over the anal sphincter, the strength of the pelvic floor, which supports the uterus and the bladder, and bladder control. Also, by increasing blood circulation in the perineum, this exercise can promote healing of the episiotomy stitches. To do the exercise, simply contract the muscles of the pelvic floor—the muscles you would use to hold back urine or a bowel movement when you have the urge to go to the bathroom. Tighten them as much as you can, hold for a count of three, and slowly release.

At first, you may not be able to feel yourself contracting these muscles because they're so stretched out of shape from birth. But if you continue to try, you'll begin to gain more control over the muscles. Your goal is to repeat the contractions seventy-five times a day everyday. As you gain more control, you'll notice that lifting the pelvic floor also tightens the muscles of the anus and the vagina which accounts for the toning effect of this exercise on those muscles.

- Abdominal strengthening: A mild abdominal exercise—holding in your stomach muscles for a count of five and releasing them—is not difficult for the new mother and can begin the process of strengthening and toning the flaccid abdominal wall, which is essential to

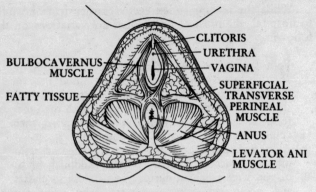

PELVIC FLOOR MUSCLE

good posture and back support. You can expect to regain bladder control after four to six weeks of regular exercise. Remember, however, that the improvement must be maintained by continued exercise.

While lying flat on your back, place your hands on your abdomen. Take a deep breath. As you exhale, draw in and tighten your abdominal muscles. At the same time press your lower back into the bed to stretch the back muscles. At first you may not notice your abdominal muscles tightening very much, but you'll feel the muscles working under your hands.

•Pelvic rock: The pelvic rock is good for strengthening the abdominals, preventing poor posture, and relieving muscular backache.

While lying flat on your back, bend your knees and place your feet flat on the bed. Keep your knees and feet together. Tighten the muscles in your buttocks and then roll up your pelvis. As you perform the pelvic tilt, tighten your abdominal muscles and press your lower back into your bed. Hold the tilt for a moment and then slowly lower your buttocks back onto the mattress. Repeat three to six times.

•Leg slides: Leg slides are good for relieving backache and preventing poor posture.

While lying flat on your back with legs extended, slide one foot up toward your buttocks, bending the

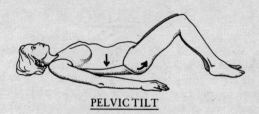

PELVIC TILT

knee. Press the small of your back into the mattress as you slide the leg out again. Then, slide the other leg up toward the buttocks, pressing the small of your back into the mattress as you extend that leg as well. Repeat the exercise five times with each leg, alternating sides.

LEG SLIDE

Usually you'll receive your exercise instructions on the first day after birth. The regimen often is built around a sequence adding a new exercise every few days after recovery.

FLUID LOSS

During pregnancy you retained more fluids than normal in your body to support the 25 percent increase in your blood volume. After birth your body will want to rid itself of the excess fluid as rapidly as possible as liquid waste. In fact, you can expect to lose several pounds of retained fluid in the first few days after birth. This accounts, then, for the seemingly endless trips to the toilet.

SWEATING

Many mothers wake up the first few nights after birth drenched in sweat. You might think that you've had a fever or are in some way ill, but this profuse sweating is a result of postpartum hormonal changes—particularly the dramatic drop in estrogen. Although profuse sweating is nothing to worry about, you will want to make sure that you have several changes of nightgowns so that there's always a dry one available if you need it.

IVs

Many women have an intravenous catheter (IV) in place during labor and delivery. The IV provides access to your veins in case emergency administration of medication or blood is needed. You can request that an IV not be placed during labor, although some physicians and hospitals require it. Certainly you should discuss your preferences with your doctor or midwife *before* you deliver your baby. The IV usually is removed on the first day. You might notice some swelling or a bruise where the needle was inserted. Numbness also is a common reaction. Warm compresses can help this area heal quickly.

BACKACHE

Backache in the first few days of recovery is a common complaint. Many women bruise their tailbones when the baby passes through the birth canal. Some even fracture the coccyx. The kind of backache that most women experience is the kind you have after you fall on your tailbone while ice skating or roller skating. It's hard to stand erect, lie flat, or sit comfortably.

There's really no aggressive treatment for these backaches. Time will take care of them. However, you can make yourself more comfortable with a rubber ring or pillows to sit on. Also, when you're lying down, try a heating pad on the area to soothe it. A bruised tailbone will heal quicker and cause less pain than a fractured one. In either case, you can ask for pain relievers to help you through the recovery.

HEADACHE

Headache is most often a symptom in women who have had spinal anesthetics. The reason for the headache is not certain, but it appears to be from continued leakage of the spinal fluid through a puncture made during the administering of the anesthesia. The leak in most instances self-corrects in a few days.

Most women notice that the headache only bothers them when they sit up and disappears completely when they are flat on their backs. It follows that treatment for this kind of headache often is in the form of prevention. Women who have spinal anesthesia often are instructed to stay flat on their backs for several hours after delivery. Fluid replacement also is important, and you will be given extra fluids either orally or intravenously after delivery. For immediate relief of the headache, you also may be offered a mild pain reliever, either through your IV or orally.

When a headache continues for several days, another therapy may be used to heal the puncture. Known as a blood patch, this treatment involves injecting blood from the mother into the site of the puncture in the spine. The blood forms a patch over the puncture, stops the spinal fluid leakage, and cures the headache in just a few hours.

FEVER

A slight elevation in temperature during the first twenty-four hours after delivery is common.

However, if your temperature rises higher than 100.4°F for any two consecutive days during the first ten days postpartum, your physician or midwife will want to do some tests to determine the cause of the fever and treat it appropriately. Common causes of postpartum fever include infection of the intrauterine cavity, urinary tract infection, and infection of the abdominal incision following Cesarean deliveries.

FREQUENTLY PRESCRIBED MEDICATIONS

During your first day and night at the hospital, the combination of soreness from stitches, backache, swelling breasts, constipation, and excitement or anxiety about your new role as a mother may make it difficult for you to rest comfortably. Rest is critical to your recovery, and your attending staff will provide you with medication to ease your discomfort and help you relax. The most common drugs used for new mothers are sedatives, painkillers, laxatives, stool softeners, antibiotics, and milk suppressants.

Most of us have been warned about side effects of drugs and the dangers of passing medication on to a baby through breast milk, so we're leery about accepting medications. The majority of medications do pass into the mother's milk in diluted amounts, and some drugs can be dangerous for the infant. However, the drugs commonly prescribed postpartum are generally safe for nursing mothers and infants. To be certain, however, you should make sure that your attending medical staff is aware that you are nursing so that medications will be prescribed in a manner that is safe for you and your baby.

Awareness of the risks of taking drugs is important, however the risks have to be weighed against the benefits to come to a meaningful decision about whether or not to take a medication. If a new mother is unable to sleep after her birth because of pain from her incision or discomfort from the contractions accompanying the uterus's involution, the benefits of taking a mild painkiller that will allow her to rest may outweigh the nominal risks of the medication.

In fact, many new mothers experience enough postpartum discomfort, from either incisions, engorged breasts, or backache, to require some form of pain relief. The drug most often used for this purpose is a mild analgesic, the most common being acetaminophen (e.g., Tylenol)—the same aspirin-free pain reliever you would use at home.

If the attending nurse or doctor feels that acetaminophen won't be strong enough to make you comfortable, he or she may suggest acetaminophen with codeine, Darvon, or Motrin to provide stronger relief. And if your pain is severe, the strong painkiller meperidine (Demerol) may be prescribed.

Tension and anxiety combined with postpartum discomfort can make sleep an elusive goal for many new mothers. Rest is critical to recovery, and if a new mother is too agitated to sleep, a sedative may be prescribed on the first night to help her get the rest she needs. Two sleeping pills, Dalmane and Seconal, are used commonly.

In the case of antibiotics, certain drugs should be avoided, and nursing mothers should ask if the one they are receiving is safe for the baby.

It would be impossible to draw up a complete list of the drugs to be avoided by nursing mothers because of the different circumstances affecting individual mothers. The list of drugs that a nursing mother may need to take in the event of an illness or recurrence of a chronic condition is indeed long. For a healthy woman with a healthy child, a drug-free nursing period is certainly the optimum. However, should an illness requiring medication arise, the mother and the doctor have to consider the age and condition of the nursing infant, the dose of medication required, and whether or not the drug pass-through poses enough of a risk to outweigh the benefits of breastfeeding. There is no one rule-of-thumb for combining drugs with nursing.

DIET AND WEIGHT LOSS

Rare is the new mother who isn't anxious to get on a scale after birth to see that her weight gain has fallen off her. Most of us have heard stories of women dropping twenty-five pounds on the delivery table or coming home weighing *less* than they weighed when they became pregnant. These fortunate women may exist, but the majority of us won't be that lucky.

Most women can expect to lose about seventeen or eighteen pounds during delivery and in the first day or two after. The weight loss breaks down like this:

Newborn	7 lb.
Placenta	1.5 lb.
Amniotic fluid	1.5 lb.
Body fluids/blood	7 lb.

Don't be surprised, however, if you weigh in at the hospital and find that you've only lost nine or ten pounds, or even less. Seventeen or eighteen pounds is the *average* weight loss. Just as some women will lose the weight more rapidly, others will lose it more slowly.

It's hard not to be terribly concerned about weight loss, especially since there's often prodding or well-meant humor from friends and relatives about getting back into shape. The postpartum woman needs to be reassured that the average new mother takes nine to twelve months to return to her original shape and weight. She should be reminded that the first few weeks after birth is not the time to worry about cutting back on calories since she may end up with a diet insufficient in the nutrients necessary to help her recover from childbirth.

WHY YOUR STOMACH ISN'T FLAT

If you went to visit your hospital labor and delivery areas before you had your baby, you might have been perplexed to see so many apparently pregnant women walking around in nightgowns. Were they there for tests?

Were they all in the early stages of labor? Now that you've had your baby, you know the answer to your questions. Just after you deliver your baby, you may look down and see a plain where a mountain was. With a sigh of relief, you welcome the sight of your old body. However, when you take your first walk the next day, more than likely you'll be surprised and disappointed to find that the swell of your pregnancy has returned and you look much like the women you'd seen when you came to visit.

Although the uterus makes a remarkably quick job of returning to its original size, it takes more than one night to do so. When you wake up the day after delivery, your uterus will still be the size it was when you were four or five months pregnant. When you're lying down, this now empty sack may appear flat. But when you stand up you'll see it bulge.

The enlarged uterus, however, is only part of the reason your stomach is so prominent. During pregnancy the muscles of your waistline and abdomen have been stretched to the limit to accommodate your growing baby. For the moment, these muscles continue to hang loosely

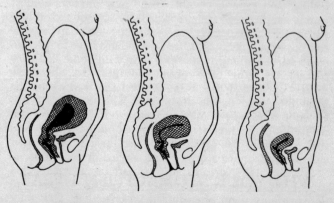

UTERUS IMMEDIATELY AFTER BIRTH   **UTERUS 1½ DAYS AFTER BIRTH**   **UTERUS SIX WEEKS AFTER BIRTH**

and add to your pregnant look, although with exercise and time they can return to their strong, flat shape.

WILD MOODS AND STRANGE VISIONS

The early postpartum period is a kind of emotional twilight zone. Most women experience mood instability. They seem quick to anger or be upset one minute and ethereally elated the next. Many report that they feel their emotions more intensely and can't summon up the normal system of checks and balances they use.

The cause for the mood shifts is thought to be the sudden drop in circulating estrogen and progesterone combined with physical exhaustion following delivery and anxiety over the new role of motherhood. The normal course for this emotional mayhem is about a week. However, as with any other part of the postpartum experience, some women feel it longer and some shorter.

Emotional instability is referred to often as a common aftereffect of childbirth. However, other more bizarre feelings and experiences that many new mothers confess to one another are rarely reported. Dreams of such intensity as to be almost visions or hallucinations are experienced by many women. Often the dreams have to do with some harm coming to the baby or with some ordinary part of the baby care routine. Mothers describe these dreams as so real that they can feel the warmth of the baby they hold in the dream even after they wake up. Often it takes several minutes to sort out the dream from reality. Some awaken from a dream about nursing to find that their milk has let down. Others awaken with their sheets bundled into a baby shape cradled in their arms.

Vivid, intense dreams are not part of the recognized catalogue of postpartum experiences, and the women who do experience them often find them unsettling. Generally they fade as the new mother's body gradually returns to its normal state and she adapts emotionally to her new life as a mother.

Intense *physical* responses to a newborn also are common. Many new mothers feel a visceral tether to their infants that makes their crying unbearable. Research now shows that the extreme uneasiness mothers feel is a built-in defense mechanism for the baby. The crying is pitched in just the right manner to make it impossible to ignore. The mother's blood pressure shoots up, her breathing becomes more rapid and her palms sweat. She can *feel* the need to stop her baby's crying.

You may wonder, "Will I feel this way when he or she is in college and homesick? How will I ever let go if I can't bear him or her to be unhappy?" Be reassured that your response will change as your child grows. It's the infant's cry that spurs a new mother to pole vault to the crib or infant seat, and that cry changes as your newborn matures into a toddler, teenager, and adult. This is not to say that you'll ever feel comfortable hearing your child cry, but you probably will lose the urgent need to whisk him or her into your arms to be comforted long before your child can ask for the keys to the car. In the meantime, listen to your body's signals. You can't spoil a newborn by picking him or her up too often. You and your baby both will be more content if you respond quickly to a cry for attention.

ROOMING-IN

Many of you will be offered the option of having your baby (and in some cases your partner) room-in with you for the duration of your hospital stay. If you choose rooming-in, your baby will be with you around-the-clock except during visiting hours, when he or she will be taken to the nursery to be bathed and examined. (The nursery-restriction during visiting hours is to protect the newborn from exposure to colds or other infections that visitors might have.)

Some women thrive on this early closeness with their newborns. Nursing mothers in particular feel that such an arrangement also increases the chances of early breastfeeding success, since they can nurse on demand rather than according to the hospital's schedule. Other women, however, exhausted and sore from a long difficult delivery, prefer to sleep or rest quietly between feedings, and to build up their strength for their return home. You may feel too worn out to have the baby with you on your first day postpartum, but ready for full time motherhood on the next. Don't hesitate to ask for a change in your routine. Many hospitals will honor a switch to rooming-in midway through the postpartum stay.

TWENTY-FOUR-HOUR DISCHARGE

Many hospitals now offer the option of a twenty-four-hour rather than a three day maternity stay. The benefits of a shorter stay include:

- Less chance of you or your baby contracting an infection from the hospital environment.
- Greater chance for you and your family to bond with your newborn.
- More uninterrupted rest for you.

Psychologically, the shorter hospital stay is beneficial also. Hospital protocol often gives new mothers the impression that they're sick rather than that they're recovering from a normal function. Leaving the hospital early gives you less time to adopt a patient mentality about childbirth.

Most new mothers can take advantage of the earlier discharge. It is inadvisable, however, under these circumstances:

- Lack of a good support system at home. If you don't have a partner, relative, or hired help to clean up, cook, and shop for you when you get home, you're probably better off taking the two- or three-day maternity stay in the hospital. In this situation, the new mother might be overstrained if she were to return home twenty-four hours after delivery.

- Excessive blood loss and requiring intravenous therapy for anemia.
- Infection.
- A baby being kept in the hospital for a day or two for observation.
- Delivery by Cesarean section or extensive surgical repair after a vaginal birth.
- Generally slow recovery.

The twenty-four-hour discharge is still an option today, but as hospital utilization committees become more stringent in the use of beds, it will probably become the rule. Since a normal postpartum recovery is not an illness requiring medical intervention, doctors will find it more and more difficult to justify keeping healthy new mothers in the hospital longer than twenty-four hours. After all, childbirth is not an illness.

The first three days after a vaginal birth can be difficult ones for the new mother. She looked forward to having her body back and getting caught up in nurturing her new child. Instead, she may find that her own physical needs compete with the needs of her baby, making the first attempts at mothering more frustrating than rewarding. However, by the end of her hospital stay, the new mother will probably feel more comfortable physically and able to enjoy holding, rocking, and feeding her baby.

For mothers who delivered by Cesarean section, the joys of motherhood may seem even more elusive. Because they need to recover both from abdominal surgery and from childbirth, these mothers are even more restricted in their early attempts at mothering. However, a little extra support from her partner and a few helpful hints from the nursing staff can make the first few days after surgical delivery less difficult, as you'll see in the next chapter.

DRAKE

Heather had to be put out completely for the delivery since the epidural wasn't taking effect as it should have. I wasn't able to be in the operating room for the delivery, which was very upsetting to me. Immediately after the surgery was completed, however, the nurse called me into the delivery room. Heather was completely out of it, so I couldn't really talk to her. I went right over to see Tucker. He was being weighed and cleaned up. I walked over and looked at him and called his name. I swear he turned and looked at me. I don't know if he really responded to me or whether it was just coincidence, but it sure gave me a good feeling.

SHARON

Once the anesthetic wore off, I had a lot of pain in the incision area. I was given injections of painkiller, and that helped, but of course it made me sleepy. I had my Cesarean in the morning, and I guess I kind of dozed through the afternoon when they brought David to me to see if I wanted to nurse. I had to lie flat on my back to prevent the headache people sometimes get after having a spinal anesthetic, but the nurse was able to raise the bed a little and then helped me find a position in which I could nurse David. Well, he was marvelous, really. Took just the smallest amount of encouragement the first time and then latched on and nursed like a pro. I had no problem in that department.

But I really couldn't move. They taught me how to raise up the bed, swing my feet over the side and use my arms to push myself up, but when I got up, I had to support my incision with one hand so it wouldn't feel as if it was ripping open, and hold onto my IV pole with the other hand, so it was a real juggling act. And I couldn't really pick David up or even adjust my position with him in bed without a lot of pain near the incision. So I really left the care of him to the nurses. They'd bring him to me bathed, powdered, and diapered. I'd nurse him. Then they'd whisk him away again to the nursery. At the time, that was all I really wanted to do with David. I was trying to cope with the aftereffects of the surgery.

I remember on the third or fourth day—the catheter was out, the IV was gone and I was eating regular meals—I walked down the hall, holding my abdomen together, to take a shower. Being able to bathe under running water was a real treat after the bed baths I'd been getting. But I was totally exhausted after the shower. I just had no energy. So nursing was really the only interaction I had with David. And I realized when I was getting ready to leave the hospital that I had never even changed him. I asked to change him before I went home, but the nurses were rushed, so one of them really diapered him for me. In the end, I left the hospital without ever having even diapered my own baby. But I caught on quick at home.

INARA

I must say that my recovery in the hospital was better than I thought it would be. I was totally exhausted after the operation. But the Cesarean section had followed a whole day of hard albeit unproductive labor, so I was tired from the operation as well as from the long labor. I had a spinal and had to lie flat on my back for about a day. My incision hurt, but I was given injections in anticipation of the pain the first day, so I didn't suffer much. Also, after going through those long hours of labor, very little felt like real pain to me. The only real problem was turning over in bed. I just couldn't do it without a burning, aching sensation in my incision. That was Wednesday evening, after I delivered Paulie. Through Thursday evening, I was pretty out of it. I did try nursing Paulie, but he was groggy and didn't have much interest at first.

I had some discomfort from gas, though not a tremendous amount. The nurses helped me get up and walk around a little, which helped get my bowels moving again. Actually, by Thursday night I was off the injections and feeling pretty good. By Friday, I felt like a whole person again. I had a little trouble getting up and down, but no discomfort nursing the baby, and no problem walking around. In fact, I was a little too active that day and ended up being exhausted and sore on Saturday from overdoing it. I'm pretty sure that the placement of the incision (I had a bikini-line incision) had a lot to do with my fast recovery.

I guess that I should also mention that I never had any regrets about the C-section. I was ready at least two hours before the doctor decided it was time to operate. There hasn't been a minute since the birth that I felt badly about the delivery. I did the best I could. I was willing and tried to have a vaginal delivery, but my body just wasn't cooperating. There's nothing I could do about that.

3

THE FIRST WEEK: CESAREAN DELIVERY

As Sharon and Inara suggest, the first day after a Cesarean section is the toughest. The post-Cesarean mother usually wakes up after her first night's rest in a strange environment, attached to intravenous tubes and a bladder catheter. Every time she tries to shift her weight, she's likely to feel pain and pulling around her incision. When the nurse knocks on her door and cheerfully presents her with the baby, this mother may dissolve into tears. She wants to hold and cuddle and nurse her new baby, but every minor shift in bed is painful. How will she be able to handle her baby?

The nurse probably knows what this new mother is thinking and will help her learn how to manage her newborn without causing herself a great deal of discomfort. The mother's partner also will play a critical part in the first couple days of parenting by bringing the baby to and from the bed, changing the position of the bed, or holding the baby while Mom shifts to a better position. It's this support from the nursing staff, doctor, and partner that will lighten the post-Cesarean mother's mood and help her enjoy her newborn despite the discomforts of postpartum and postsurgical symptoms.

This new mother in particular needs to know what kind of sensations she can expect to have after birth, how she can cope with them to make her hospital stay as comfortable as possible, and how long the painful aftereffects of a Cesarean section will last. She needs to feel that sometime in the future she'll be able to cradle and walk her baby just like the mother in the next bed who delivered vaginally.

Every woman who delivers by Cesarean section will have a different recovery experience, and she can expect to have reactions that fall into a broad category of normal experiences. It's important to remember that part of her recovery will follow the same path as that of the new mother who delivers vaginally. The post-Cesarean mother's uterus will involute, a bloody discharge will follow delivery, and the shift in hormones will occur, often causing some mood swings during the first week or so after delivery. All of these aspects of postpartum recovery are covered in Chapter 2, "The First Three Days." So make sure to read that chapter regardless of the kind of delivery you experienced.

Of course, there are special considerations for the mother who delivers by Cesarean section. Her surgery complicates the recovery from childbirth. Below is a guide to the most common sensations following surgical delivery. Keep in mind when reading through the guide that every woman will respond differently to her delivery. The mother who labored for many hours and then was wheeled into the delivery room for an emergency Cesarean section may be more exhausted and recover more slowly than the mother for whom the decision for a surgical delivery was made early in labor. Also, some women feel more discomfort than others, and that will affect their mood and recovery. As a result, some new mothers may hardly notice the sensations mentioned below, while others will remember them as painful episodes in their recoveries.

POSTSURGICAL SORENESS

The first twenty-four to thirty-six hours after a Cesarean are generally the most difficult. Many women report a general soreness in the abdominal and pelvic area. A lot of that soreness is due to the abdominal muscles running vertically from chest cage to pelvis (the recti muscles), which were stretched and pulled aside in order to reach the uterus. Most of us have pulled a muscle at one time or another. You know how sore and swollen it feels. That's the same sensation you'll have in your abdomen where the muscles were manually pulled and separated during the surgery. As with any other pulled muscles, the soreness is most severe for the first couple of days and decreases in intensity thereafter.

INCISION DISCOMFORT

The incisions made during the Cesarean section are actually five or six layers deep, cutting through the outer skin and several inner layers, including muscle. Each layer has its own set of stitches. The internal stitches will be made of materials that dissolve in the course of several weeks. The surface incision, however, may be sutured with removable stitches, dissolving stitches, or simply stapled together. If the stitches are removable, or if staples were used, they will be taken out after a few days, when the incision has healed enough to remain closed, and a dressing may be applied over the incision.

The tissue around the sutures or staples probably will become inflamed and swollen in the processes of healing. As a result, the incision often is quite painful in the first day or two. You'll be offered either Demerol or morphine by injection to ease the pain. If you need it, take it. Some women get so caught up in the argument against drugs during childbirth that they carry on the fight even after they've had a Cesarean. However, keep in mind that unnecessary pain can be detrimental both to you and to your baby for several reasons:

- The discomfort can keep the new mother from resting comfortably after her delivery, and rest is the key to recovering quickly and getting to the main order of business: Mothering.
- Pain also can keep you from moving, another important part of early recovery. You need to change position in bed, sit up, and even walk around the first couple of days. Movement helps encourage good cir-

culation, which is important in preventing the formation of blood clots and swelling of the blood vessels in the legs. Good circulation also brings blood to the incision and promotes healing. And moving encourages deeper breathing, which helps clear the lungs after surgery and prevent pneumonia.

•A normal reaction to pain is tension. You're bracing against the pain. Your baby can feel you stiffen when you feel a sharp pain. Your tension and discomfort will be obvious in the way you hold and handle him or her. Babies are sensitive to the manner in which they are handled and often fret when they sense tension in the person holding them. A painkiller can make your first attempts at mothering easier for you and your newborn.

•Pain can interfere with early attempts at nursing, also. Once again, the culprit is tension. The first few attempts at nursing often take patience and a lot of shifting around to find a comfortable position for the mother and the baby. A mother in a lot of pain will be too tense to have much patience or to be able to find a good position for nursing. Her baby also may pick up on the tension and begin to fuss, which will only further aggravate the situation.

Once the breastfeeding is successful, the new mother also has to cope with the sometimes sharp contractions (nursing cramps) that occur as a part of involution while the baby suckles. Because of the incision, these contractions might feel very painful for the post-Cesarean mother, and the pain medication will take the edge off them enough to allow her to relax during her nursing sessions.

Pain medication by injection probably will be offered to you only for the first day or two until you can start to eat, are feeling better, and can take milder forms of painkillers, such as acetaminophen (e.g., Tylenol) with codeine. Nursing need not be interrupted while taking painkillers in the usual therapeutic doses. The baby may become more sleepy from the medication passed on to him or her in the breast milk, but this effect will not last.

BLADDER CONTROL

Because of the surgical procedure as well as the anesthesia used during a Cesarean section, the bladder tends to be insensitive to fullness during the first hours after delivery. All women are catheterized during the operation and for their immediate postoperative recovery. The catheter usually is removed the first day on the maternity ward and the new mother is encouraged to try to go to the bathroom—even if she doesn't feel like it.

Bladder sensitivity will return in the first couple of days, but during that time your nurse will occasionally feel your bladder externally by pressing on your abdomen with her hand to make sure that you're not retaining urine; a distended, full bladder is an invitation for a bladder infection.

BOWEL FUNCTION

During the Cesarean section, your bowel will probably be moved aside in the process of delivering the baby. The handling of the bowel, its exposure to air, and the effects of the anesthetic probably will bring its function pretty much to a halt. You probably will not have eaten or drunk very much in the past day either, so there's nothing to encourage activity in the bowel after surgery. Because of these circumstances, gas may collect in the sluggish bowel and be released slowly or not at all. We've all had transient sharp gas pains on occasion, but as the gas moves through the bowel, the pain dissipates. In the post-Cesarean mother, however, the gas moves very little. It collects in the bowel and can cause painful gas cramps during the second or third day.

A couple of preventive measures may help minimize the pain by preventing gas build-up and promoting its passage.

•Steer clear of carbonated drinks or liquids that might promote the formation of gas, such as milk products.

•Drink warm liquids that stimulate the bowel.
•Try to walk around as much as you're allowed. Movement helps get the bowel going again, which in turn helps you pass the gas rather than allow it to build up.
•When you're in bed, change positions often. Lie on one side with knees up and then change to the other side. Again, shifting positions in gentle movement, which will help stimulate the bowel.

If you find yourself in a lot of discomfort despite these preventive measures, you have several avenues of treatment to try. First, a chewable tablet or liquid containing simethicone may be prescribed. Simethicone breaks the bigger gas bubbles into smaller gas bubbles, which are easier to pass through the bowel. Once the gas enters the lower rectal area, you may be offered a Harris flush if the gas still won't pass through the rectum. The Harris flush is a simple procedure during which a tube is inserted into the rectum and water is flushed in and out of the lower bowel. When the water comes out, the gas frequently comes out with it.

Other avenues of treatment include rectal suppositories or enemas, both of which encourage movement in the bowel and, therefore, facilitate the passing of gas.

DIET

Unlike mothers who deliver vaginally, post-Cesarean mothers will not be put on a regular diet. Most physicians keep their postoperative patients on a liquid diet until they are able to pass intestinal gas without the aid of medications, suppositories, or enemas. The natural passing of gas is an indication that the bowel has recovered from the surgery and/or anesthesia and is ready to function normally.

Normal bowel function usually is restored in two to three days. Most mothers aren't terribly hungry for the first twenty-four to thirty-six hours, but after that they might feel as if they're being systematically starved. Rest assured, however, that by the third day you'll be able to eat some solid food, and by the end of the week you should be on a normal diet.

INVOLUTION

The uterus of the post-Cesarean mother contracts to its original size in the same manner as that of the mother who has delivered vaginally. The contractions of the uterus begin after delivery and can be quite painful owing to the incision in the abdomen. During the first day, the progress of the involution will be checked by the nurse, who will press on the uterus to make sure that it is firm. This examination also can be painful but only lasts for a few seconds.

The painkillers offered for postsurgical discomfort will help the mother cope with the strong early contractions of the involution process. By the time she is comfortable enough to forgo pain medication, the contractions will be less uncomfortable, except during nursing sessions.

NURSING

A Cesarean delivery does not in any way affect your body's milk-producing ability. The hormonal changes that initiate milk production will occur whether you deliver vaginally or by Cesarean section. A problem you may encounter, however, is finding a nursing style that is physically comfortable. Mothers who have the lower "bikini" cut often have an easier time than those whose incision runs the length of their lower abdomen because they experience less direct pressure on the incision while nursing. In either case, however, a pillow placed under the baby will both help support the baby and cushion the incision at the same time.

Picking up and putting down the baby also can present a problem since lifting anything the first few days after a Cesarean can pull painfully on the incision. You can count on a nurse to bring your baby during the hospital's regularly scheduled feeding hours, but you can't always count on having your baby taken out of your arms when you're finished nursing. Try to have your partner available to help you either rest the baby by your side or move him or her back to the bassinet when you're finished nursing. You might also need a hand in burping your newborn between breasts and after the feeding.

POSTPARTUM DISCHARGE

Even though the doctor often sponges out the uterus and makes sure that the placenta is removed completely after the delivery, mothers who deliver by Cesarean will have the normal postpartum bloody discharge, or lochia. The discharge may be lighter because of the post-delivery swabbing, but as the uterus contracts there will still be some flow as the uterine wall where the placenta was attached heals.

Most often you'll be given a large sanitary napkin to wear with a belt. The belt may be uncomfortable for you to wear over your incision. If so, you might want to try wearing a self-adhesive pad in full-size panties that fit easily over your abdomen. These do have a tendency to slip more than a pad attached to a sanitary belt, so leaking can be more of a problem. However, that often is a small price to pay for the added comfort.

SITTING AND STANDING

Post-Cesarean mothers often have difficulties moving because they habitually use their abdominal muscles to help pull themselves up or ease themselves down. Part of your week in the hospital will be spent learning how to shift yourself without relying on your stomach muscles. Though you can ask the nurse for help and rely on your electric bed while in the hospital, you'll need to know how to maneuver without these aids when you go home. Now is a good time to practice so that you can get assistance when you need it.

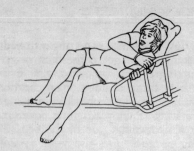

**USE ELBOWS OR SIDE
TO PULL UP**

SLIDE OFF THE BED

**USE ARMS TO PUSH UP TO
A STANDING POSITION**

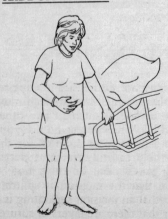

**SUPPORT INCISION
WITH ONE ARM**

The biggest maneuvering problems are getting into bed and out of bed to get the baby or go to the bathroom. One common solution is to get up in two steps.

First, raise the bed to a sitting position. You can do this yourself if you have an electric bed, or ask your nurse to do it if you have a crank bed. Push yourself up on your elbows and swing your feet over the side of the bed so that you are in a sitting position. Or, use your raised bedrail for support while you pull yourself into a sitting position with legs over the side of the bed. Relax for a minute and take a deep breath.

Second, using your arms at your side, slide yourself off the bed and onto your feet. If a stepping stool is available, it might make this step easier.

When you want to get back into bed, just reverse the procedure. Use your arms—rather than your abdominal muscles—as support to ease yourself into a sitting position. Then, using the raised bedrail for support, bend your legs back on the bed. Ease yourself back to your sitting position with your arms and adjust your bed to a comfortable position.

It will take some time to learn *not* to use your abdominals, so don't be put off by early unsuccessful or semi-successful attempts. The first few times you get out of bed, you'll be under the watchful eye of a nurse, who can lend an arm if you get in an uncomfortable position.

THE FIRST POSTOPERATIVE STEPS

Even with your nurse's careful attention, standing up for the first time will probably be an unpleasant surprise. Your uterus will still be enlarged and your stomach muscles stretched out of shape and weak, just as any other postpartum mother's would be. When you stand up, your abdomen will bulge out and provide no support for the incision, so the tissue in the area will stretch. It's this tugging on the incision that causes pain. You also may be frightened by the sensation that the incision is splitting open. However, be assured that an incision separating is a rare occurrence. Remember that there are layers of sutures holding the tissues together, not just the staples or stitches you see on the surface. If that thought doesn't assuage your fears, take a look your incision while you're on your feet. Once you see that it feels terrible but looks fine, you may be encouraged to move more bravely.

You'll be encouraged to get out of bed and walk around for a few minutes the day after your delivery. Your first trips may only be to the bathroom and back, but even those short trips will be difficult. Because of the painful pulling that often occurs when you stand up, you may try to favor your incision by hunching over and shuffling from place to place. Your nurse, however, will seem unsympathetic to your discomfort and insist that you stand up straight despite the pain it causes. What she knows, and you need to know, is that crouching over will not help and may even hurt you in the long run. If you give in to the urge to stoop over protectively during the first few days, you'll reduce blood circulation to the incision when increased blood circulation is needed to promote healing. Also, you'll find that the healing tissues will become stiff in this hunched attitude and straightening up will be even more painful and difficult as time goes on.

Some women find that the whole process of learning how to stand up and maneuver is easier if they are given some kind of binding to support the abdomen and the incision. While this may be helpful in the first few days, it's wise not to become too dependent on it. You need to get your own abdominal strength back gradually by consciously holding in your muscles while walking or standing. If you get used to your binder doing all of the work, you might not make the effort to regain your abdominal muscle tone yourself. Before asking for a binder, try bracing your incision with your pillow during transitional movements. You'll have the support when you need it but will be able to start depending on your own muscles the rest of the time.

POSTOPERATIVE EXERCISE

A lot of post-Cesarean mothers probably wonder why they should move at all if it hurts so much. It seems much more natural just to lie in bed and wait to feel better. Surely rest is an important part of recovery, but mild exercise is equally important.

Walking, for instance, improves circulation in the legs and prevents blood clots from forming. It also encourages circulation in the area of the incision, which promotes healing. Even in the more comfortable reclining position, however, the post-Cesarean mother should do some gentle exercises that will prevent circulatory problems in her legs, keep her lungs clear of mucus, and encourage her bowel to become more active.

During surgery—especially when general anesthesia is used—respiration is slowed down, and there's a chance that mucus and fluid will collect in the lungs. If lungs are not cleared properly after surgery, there's a risk of infection, such as the development of pneumonia. For this reason you'll be asked to cough frequently to clear your lungs. However, coughing can be very painful after abdominal surgery. Many mothers try to cough but do so too gently to help clear out the lungs. "Huffing," described below, can be as effective as coughing but will cause much less discomfort.

HUFFING Huffing is simply the forceful passage of air from the lungs. It's like coughing, but puts much less strain on the abdominal muscles—and on your sore incision. To do this exercise, open your mouth and let your jaw go slack. Take a deep breath. Then, supporting your incision with a pillow or your hands, forcefully push the air out of your lungs. Saying "Ha" on exhalation may help. Most of the effort should come from your diaphragm, not your abdomen. Don't be surprised if you "huff" up mucus from your lungs. That's the purpose of the exercise. Just spit it into a tissue or cup and discard it. Huffing can be repeated once or twice an hour in the first day or two after surgery.

LEG SLIDES   This exercise strengthens the abdominals, which will help support your incision when you're on your feet. It also stimulates the bowel, which helps prevent or relieve post-operative gas pains. Lying prone or in a semi-reclining position, bend one leg, bringing the foot as close to the buttocks as possible and then stretching it out straight again. Bend and stretch the other leg in the same manner. Repeat three to five times. (See illustration p. 43)

PELVIC TILT   This is another exercise that will help your lower intestine return to normal function. Bend your legs at the knees keeping your feet flat on the bed. Gently roll up your lower spine and then roll it down until your back is flat on the bed again. Repeat three times. (See illustration p. 43)

VISITORS

In most cases your friends and relatives would give you a day or two of benign neglect to recuperate from major surgery. However, most people view Cesarean delivery more as childbirth and less as major surgery. The throngs approach practically as you're wheeled into your room from recovery. For some, these visitors are a great help, boosting the spirits, taking the mind off incision discomfort, IVs, and liquid diets. However, for many mothers the endless parade of visitors with candy, flowers, and stories about *their* friends who had C-sections is exhausting. If you fit into the latter group, here are a few suggestions for cutting down on the crowd:

- Keep your door closed and have a note posted on it saying "Visits limited to ten minutes." The closed door is less inviting than the open one, and the sign alerts visitors that you're recuperating and need more rest than company.
- Ask your partner to instruct well-wishers over the phone to postpone their visit until you get home.

This device can cut down on a great deal of your room traffic.

•Don't be bashful about telling guests that you are tired and would like to rest.

•For visitors who stay on despite your request for privacy, establish a code with your partner that will signal when you want him to take guests on a baby-viewing mission to get them out of the room and on their way home.

POST-CESAREAN FEELINGS

Childbirth, regardless of how it's accomplished, gives rise to a spectrum of feelings including joy, confusion, apprehensiveness, weepiness, and protectiveness, partially because becoming a mother is an emotional milestone, and partially because of the hormonal changes brought on after delivery. For the mother who delivered by Cesarean, the range of emotions may be broader and perhaps felt more intensely because of the added stress of major surgery.

In the first day or two after surgery, the new mother will be plagued by her own aches and pains that prevent her from rocking, walking, and snuggling with her baby as freely as she wants. Her baby may even fret when held because it senses the tension in the mother caused by the discomfort of lifting and holding the newborn. These first difficulties with mothering can clash so with the images of nurturing before delivery that the new mother becomes distraught and depressed.

As mentioned before, encouragement and attention from the hospital staff and partner can do wonders to ease the postoperative mother's anxieties and disappointments in the first few days. The staff, however, will probably be too overburdened to take initiative beyond the routine care they would give a post-Cesarean patient. It's the partner who really needs to seek out ways to make mothering easier and more pleasant for the first few days. Make sure that she's getting the attention she needs: Is there water for her to drink? Does she have the help she asks for getting in and out of bed? Is she getting prompt pain relief? Are the nurses helping her find comfortable ways to hold the baby while nursing or bottlefeeding? Is the phone close enough for easy use? These are just a few of the needs the partner can make sure are being met.

The partner also can make mothering more pleasant by being available to share parenting duty in the hospital. When the partner is in the room, the postoperative mother can have the baby brought to her to hold and she can feel secure that if her newborn needs to be carried or rocked someone will be available on the spot to help. She doesn't have to worry about how long it will take for someone to come and help her comfort her infant.

The doctor also has an important role to play in assuaging feelings of inadequacy and disappointment in the new mother. Most pregnant women today are instructed in some method of childbirth preparation all of which presuppose a vaginal delivery. The object of these classes is to build up confidence and enthusiasm for the difficult task of labor and delivery. However, if a mother truly is looking forward to a vaginal birth, an emergency Cesarean can be not only a disappointment but in her mind a sign of inadequacy—as if she didn't prepare or perform well enough.

The post-Cesarean mother needs her doctor to review the delivery with her. Often times the memory of why a Cesarean was necessary is foggy after the surgery and postoperative recovery. The physician can help the new mother understand that she didn't "cop out" of the ordeal of labor and delivery to have a C-section. Rather, a threat to the life of her baby and/or herself demanded the procedure. Certainly, facing up to abdominal surgery and coping with a postpartum recovery complicated by the aftermath of surgery takes no less courage than experiencing vaginal delivery.

Also, the new mother can be reassured that the old adage of "Once a Cesarean, always a Cesarean" isn't true any longer. Because of advances in Cesarean procedures and in maternal and fetal monitoring techniques, most women who have had a Cesarean will be able to labor and deliver vaginally in a subsequent pregnancy.

As the end of the hospital stay nears, you may have a

sense of foreboding rather than relief. You still are weak and sore. During the hours you spent in your room with the baby, you began to realize the enormity of your newborn's needs. The whole day and night seemed completely taken up with feedings, changings, bathings, burpings, and soothings. But you always could call on the hospital staff to handle the routine care as well as to serve you meals, clean the dishes, and even give you a bath. How will you be able to attend to your newborn and find the time you need to get better yourself when you're on your own? A good solution to that problem will take some time to work out, and you're likely to have some rocky moments until you've got the kind of help you need when you need it. Some ground rules for a smooth transition are presented in the next chapter, where you'll find advice on making the first few weeks at home less exhausting and more enjoyable.

PART 2
THE FIRST
SIX WEEKS

STEVE

I remember when I took Willie home. It was an incredible high. Normally I keep to myself. But in the hospital lobby I saw someone from my neighborhood whom I'd never even met and went up to introduce myself. "Hello, I know you from the neighborhood. My wife just had a baby." It was like I was friends with everyone.

SUSAN

My baby was born prematurely and had to stay at the hospital for about two weeks, so I had to go home without her. There was a cloud over those two weeks. I was very depressed. It was hard going home empty-handed. At home the little crib was all set up for her, and all I could do was wait and see if she was going to pull through all right. I couldn't nurse her at the hospital because the nurses said that she was too weak to suck well. However, I wanted to make sure that I could nurse once she was at home, so I rented an electric breast pump—my iron baby, as I called it. I'd use the pump every four hours, even at night, just as if I were nursing my baby. Nights were the hardest. I had to get up to nurse the iron baby when I knew that other moms were nestling up with their new babies. I'd have trouble falling back to sleep again, worrying about Serena. Wondering if she'd be okay. But the milk I pumped was fed to Serena, and that made me feel good.

During the days I'd be all right. I'd visit Serena for a few hours. I could have stayed all day, but what was the point? The nurses were very fussy about her. After a few minutes they'd take her away from me, saying that she was getting cold, and put her back in the incubator. So after a couple of hours I went home and organized the house more. And when I ran out of things to organize for the baby, I'd have a chance to nap. Actually, because I didn't have a newborn at home those first couple of weeks, I had a chance to rest up a lot and recover from the birth. I was probably in better shape than most moms when Serena came home two weeks later. But the waiting and wondering and having to visit Serena at the hospital every day—that was awful.

MEG

I remember that I wasn't real keen on going home. I had a huge episiotomy and didn't really feel able to take care of myself. I was very happy that the staff fed me and took care of my baby, only bringing him in to nurse and play with me. I also was pleased that the baby could be fed in the middle of the night without disturbing me. I was just exhausted and always left the 2 AM feedings to the nursery staff, even though I was nursing the rest of the time. So I was a little apprehensive going home. Even lifting the baby was difficult because my episiotomy hurt so much.

Fortunately, my husband was at home for a couple of weeks. I would take my pillow to wherever I was going to nurse and arrange myself on it so that I was comfortable. Then my husband would bring me the baby. I knew that nursing brought on cramps, so I was prepared for that. I also wasn't surprised by the soreness of my nipples. Again, according to what I had read, that was par for the course. I remember that for a few weeks the first minute or so when the baby would latch on would be almost unbearable. But after those first seconds the pain went away, as did the cramps. And as the weeks wore on, all of the discomforts seemed to lessen.

MARIE

I was very uncomfortable for the first few weeks. I had to move slowly and deliberately to avoid increasing the discomfort I felt from my episiotomy. My breasts also were engorged quite a bit and my nipples sore from nursing every two hours. These physical aches, however, didn't take away from my immense satisfaction with motherhood. I didn't want any nurse or relative to stay with me once my husband returned to work because I was so happy to have time by myself with my new son. I spent long moments just looking at him, and singing and talking to him. Those few weeks I had with him with no other responsibilities—before I went back to work—really gave me a chance to immerse myself in my new role.

4

GOING HOME

The first six weeks of motherhood for Susan, Meg, and Marie were so different that they sound like unrelated experiences. That's what makes early motherhood so hard to generalize about. The specific problems and joys felt by every mother are unique to her particular circumstances. Some new mothers, like Susan, have to wait for their newborns to come home with them because of some medical problem. Others, like Marie, who have minimal postpartum symptoms, seem to slip into their new role with ease. And still others, like Meg, are beset by physical problems that make even the most basic attempts at mothering difficult.

Despite painful reminders of a difficult birth, though, most new mothers, even those with painful reminders of their deliveries, share a deep satisfaction in feeding the newborn and watching the baby grow in leaps and bounds in the first few weeks. Many mothers don't mind the middle-of-the-night feedings because they provide another opportunity to be close to this little miracle, to watch how the hands rest on the bottle or breast, to wonder at the intent gaze that rests on the mother's face during feedings, and to look over and over again at the perfection of the feet and toes and ears and every other part of this person made cell by cell inside the mother's body.

In the first six weeks you'll be asked about the details of your birth by family and friends and friends of friends. Even as you begin your story for what feels like the millionth time, you'll be as engrossed in the tale of your labor, delivery, and hospital stay as if it were the first time you talked about it. How terrifying, thrilling, and momentous those few days were! Reliving the birth as you talk about it over and over somehow helps you capture the experience and commit it to memory.

You and your partner also may reflect on your pregnancy, trying to match up the fetal movements inside the womb with the movements the baby makes now in the bassinet. ("Remember how we used to be able to make out her foot pressing against your belly? That's probably what she was doing in there.")

Outside the restrictions of the hospital, you, your partner, and your baby learn to function as a family. Slowly in these first few weeks your baby begins to learn about life outside the womb. You as parents become experts at discerning hungry cries from wet cries, diapering, nail clipping, bathing, feeding, soothing, and, at best, sharing these duties so that the strains of early parenthood don't fall too heavily on one partner.

The strains of early parenthood usually fall particularly hard on the new mother, however, no matter how they are shared. You'll probably still be beset by postpartum discomfort and always feel exhausted when you get home. Before you were a mother, you would have taken to bed until you felt better. But you're finding that the demands of caring for a newborn preclude the luxury of uninterrupted rest. For the most part you probably won't mind the new demands. Every time you feed, hold, rock, or bathe the baby, you're likely to fall in love with him or her anew.

LEAVING THE HOSPITAL

New mothers have varied feelings about leaving the hospital. The mother who had the attention she desired from the nurses, saw her baby as often as she wanted, liked the food, and got enough rest might not be all that anxious to go home. After all, once she leaves the hospital bed, she'll be responsible at least in part for all of the functions filled by the hospital staff. If she's having a bad day, there'll be no one to whisk away the baby for a diaper change and then put dinner on a plate in front of her. Many new mothers worry if their tiny baby will survive without the experienced attention of the nursery staff.

Mothers who have not had the attention they thought was warranted and who felt cheated of their baby's company, however, might be anxious to leave and return home, where they can have more control over their surroundings. Some may be able to leave as soon as twenty-four hours after delivery, depending on postpartum conditions and hospital policy.

However you feel about leaving the hospital, you would be wise to give some thought to the transition between maternity ward and home. What are the conveniences and comforts available at the hospital and how can they be replicated at home? The night before your expected discharge, you should make a list of things the hospital provided that you'll need at home:

- A back rest, to make nursing in bed more comfortable.
- A supply of Tucks pads and/or anesthetic spray as well as your peri-bottle to relieve discomfort caused by hemorrhoids and episiotomy stitches.
- Mild painkillers if you still need them. Is the prescription filled and available to you?
- A supply of stool softeners on hand if they were a help in the hospital.
- A sitz bath. Usually, you'll be able to take home the disposable sitz bath you use in the hospital, but ask a nurse if that's the case. If not, make sure your partner purchases one for you before you leave the hospital.
- A supply of sanitary pads.

These are some of the more common items used for hygiene and comfort; however, every new mother has problems and solutions specific to her postpartum condition. It's important to tailor the take-home list to meet your individual needs.

TAKING CARE OF BABY

A concern you're likely to share with many other new parents leaving the hospital is how you're going to keep your baby alive given your total lack of experience in childcare. To assuage some of that apprehension, make sure that you and/or your partner take the childcare class offered by your hospital before you go home. The classes usually walk new parents through the normal routines of a newborn, including feeding, burping, bathing, dressing, and diapering. Take notes if you think they will help and also take the opportunity to ask any questions about baby care that you might have.

Of course watching an expert diaper, burp, and bathe a baby is different from tending to your own. Before you leave, you might want to make arrangements for a nurse with whom you have had good rapport to watch you change, swaddle, hold, burp, and feed the baby just for that added assurance that you're a perfectly capable parent.

Make sure that you're well stocked with baby equipment before you come home, too:

Are there enough blankets, t-shirts, stretchies to last for a couple of weeks while the new family gets its bearings? In all likelihood you'll be changing your newborn several times in a day, so make sure you have a few changes of clothes and ready access to a washer and dryer. You'll probably need to do at least one load of baby wash a day.

If you're using disposable diapers, buy a supply that will last a couple of weeks. (Figure on changing the baby an average of once every two hours.) If you're using cloth diapers, have a couple dozen on hand, and if you're using a diaper service, have your partner arrange a delivery the day *before* you get home.

Whether you're bottle or breastfeeding, make sure you have an adequate supply of bottles at home. If you're bottlefeeding, keep six to eight bottles on hand so that you or your partner can prepare a day's supply at one time and refrigerate them. If you're nursing, two or three bottles plus a small stash of formula is useful in the event of an emergency which would prevent you from feeding the baby yourself. Also, expressed milk (see "Milk Expression," p. 104) in a bottle or one bottle of formula a day will allow your baby to become used to both bottle and breast, giving you some flexibility later on. (Your partner will appreciate the chance to feed the baby with the bottle, too.)

What kind of formula should you buy? Ask your pediatrician during hospital rounds and have your partner buy a supply.

If you're nursing, you'll want a supply of disposable and cotton breast shields at home so that you can try both kinds and determine which suits you better. You'll also need some pullover tops which provide the easiest and best cover when you're nursing.

Line up a few neighbors and/or relatives who you can call with emergency grocery or baby shopping lists without feeling like a burden.

VISITORS

Well-wishers and long lost relatives will probably descend on you in droves, but you're going to be in no mood for entertaining. Your postpartum fatigue is a real reason to keep visits short, so have your partner emphasize your need for rest to guests before they arrive. Also, make sure you're not put in the position of having to serve guests or clean up after them. If visitors want to come near mealtimes, suggest that they bring takeout food. Stock up on disposable dinnerware to make cleaning up as effortless as possible. And when you've had enough, excuse yourself and retire to another room. Your partner can show the guests out if they want to linger for a few moments after your exit.

RECOVERY PROGRESS

Below is an overview of the physical changes that occur in this stage of postpartum recovery. You'll also find some suggestions for minimizing common discomforts in order to make these first six weeks of discovery enjoyable and memorable.

VAGINAL DISCHARGE The lochia will fade from reddish brown to brown to yellow in three to six weeks after birth. In the first week or two you may pass some blood clots. Dark clots that are unaccompanied by a lot of bright red bleeding are normal. These usually are caused by blood pooling in the vagina, while you are sitting or lying down. The blood begins to clot in the vagina and the clot is passed when you get up and move.

If no infection is present, you won't feel any irritation or itching. However, some women do notice a strong meaty odor accompanying the discharge, especially in the first couple of weeks. The odor is part of the healing process and is probably caused by the dead tissue being sloughed off in the uterus along with the blood.

If your discharge is foul-odored and causes itching and irritation, you may have a vaginal infection. Contact your doctor or midwife for instructions about what to do.

EPISIOTOMY HEALING The new mother may still have some discomfort when she goes home at the end of her hospital stay. The same relief measures used in the hospital can be used at home: Tucks pads placed over the stitches, topical sprays, ice packs, and sitz baths. Some women find that exposing the stitches to the stream of a hot shower is very soothing.

The stitches will be absorbed by the body in ten days to four weeks. You should be fairly comfortable by your second or third week postpartum. This is not to say that the area will feel like it did before your delivery. It won't. The perineum may still be sore if stretched, but it shouldn't prevent you from going about your daily routine.

If the episiotomy is still giving you enough discomfort to make sitting and standing difficult after two weeks or so, you should have your doctor or midwife check to make sure it is healing correctly.

CESAREAN INCISIONS Your incision will still be in the early stages of healing when you return home. Often it is taped closed with an adhesive that gradually comes off in two or three weeks. Most women do not have a dressing (gauze pads and tape) on their incision when they return home unless some specific problem has developed following surgery. If you do return home with a dressing, you'll be given specific instructions about caring for your incision.

You probably will be instructed to rest and nap frequently for the first week or two, though you should *not* stay in bed. Getting up and about is important to your recovery also.

Getting in and out of bed without the aid of the electric hospital bed will be a challenge at first. Try rolling over on your side with your legs bent and using your arms to push yourself into a sitting position with legs dangling over the side. Keep a foot stool next to the bed just as you did at the hospital and push yourself off the bed with one arm, using the other hand to brace your incision. You may need some help getting up and down for a couple days, until you can maneuver without causing too much tugging on your incision. Keep a bell by your bed to signal for some help getting up and down.

Gradually the incision will feel less tender and ache less when you are standing and sitting. However, it will continue to cause twinges when you use your abdominal muscles and may do so for many months.

Although many practitioners do not consider shaving or "prepping" the site of the Cesarean incision, others continue the practice as part of the Cesarean procedure. If you had your abdomen shaved for your Cesarean, you'll probably notice the hair around the site of the incision starting to grow back in; the stubble can be irritating for a week or two. If the stubble makes the incision itchy, try not to scratch it. And if you just *have* to scratch, do so gently near the incision rather than on the incision itself. You'll get some relief without further irritating the area.

The incision itself may itch as it heals. Again, scratch around it or even try scratching an area nearby. You'd be surprised how scratching near, but not on, the site of the itch can bring relief. To reduce itching, wear cotton briefs rather than nylon underwear and stay away from nylon pantyhose. Synthetic fibers tend to exacerbate irritation in some women.

You also may notice as the weeks pass that even though the incision isn't as sore as it used to be, your abdomen doesn't feel the way it should either. Remember that many nerve endings were cut when the incision into your abdomen was made. These cut nerves take longer to heal than the incision itself, and your abdomen won't feel "normal" until the nerves are healed.

If your incision becomes more instead of less inflamed or forms a pocket where the skin is no longer meeting, have your practitioner examine it.

HEMORRHOIDS If you developed hemorrhoids during pregnancy or during delivery, they may still be swollen and painful when you're discharged from the hospital. The same soothing treatments recommended for perineal discomfort are recommended for hemorrhoid discomfort—sitz baths, running a stream of hot water over the area, Tucks pads, and topical sprays. Remember to keep hemorrhoid tissues clean and dry. If needed, continue to use a stool softener such as the kind used in the hospital. Stool softeners can make the process of elimination much less uncomfortable. They also will prevent

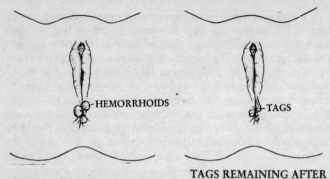

SWOLLEN HEMORRHOIDS

TAGS REMAINING AFTER HEMORRHOIDS HEAL

you from straining during a movement. Straining will only increase the irritation of the hemorrhoid tissues and prolong the discomfort they caused.

Over the next few weeks these swollen veins will shrink down to small tags, which won't cause discomfort unless you are on your feet for long periods, have diarrhea, or are constipated, at which times the hemmorhoids may swell up again.

> See your doctor if you find that your hemorrhoids are not healing or are becoming more inflamed and uncomfortable.

PHYSICAL LIMITATIONS

The first six weeks postpartum is the traditional recuperation period, after which the new mother is considered medically recovered from her delivery. Some women recover faster, however, and some recover slower. Many women who delivered vaginally continue to have vaginal discomfort after the six weeks have passed. Although annoying, this discomfort is no cause for alarm since the time it takes for an episiotomy or vaginal tears to heal completely varies from one woman to the next.

During the first six weeks, the new mother will have certain limitations on her activities. Some of the limitations will be self-imposed just because of the discomfort still felt as a result of bruised tailbones, episiotomy repairs, and C-section incisions. Many mothers also just find themselves too tired to carry on much activity other than taking care of the baby. Other activity limitations will be set by the doctor to ensure recovery in the six weeks after the delivery. The following are the routine postpartum restraints on physical activity:

VAGINAL BIRTHS   After a vaginal birth your doctor probably will tell you not to do any strenuous exercise or housecleaning for the first six weeks. Your efforts in the first few weeks should be centered on taking care of your baby and yourself.

Some doctors use the flow of lochia to determine when a new mother is overextending herself. While heavier lochia may indicate an increase in activity, it is not necessarily bad or dangerous. How the new mother *feels* is a better indication of whether or not she's too active physically.

The warning signs you should recognize are
- Soreness and fatigue. You should be feeling better from one week to the next, not worse. If you find yourself more achy and exhausted, cut down on your activities.
- Voluminous bleeding. If you're soaking two sanitary napkins in a half hour, call your doctor.

CESAREAN DELIVERY   After a Cesarean section, most new mothers aren't going to feel much like going back to their old routines. They'll tire easily just from the strain of caring for the baby. Any real exertion may cause painful pulling and aching around the incision. The exhaustion and the pain serve as good reminders for postsurgical moms to keep activity to a minimum—an important part of their recovery.

Despite these natural warnings against too much exertion, many physicians offer the following guidelines for limiting activities during the first six weeks to speed the postsurgical mother's recovery and prevent her from inadvertently disturbing the healing incision. Remember, however, that these are guidelines. Some women will feel stronger and more able to increase their activities sooner, while others may need more time to get back on their feet.

First, slowly increase the use of stairs, starting with one up and down flight a day for the first couple of weeks. Since many babies' rooms are located on the second floor of the house, this rule makes some duplication of equipment necessary. Make sure that you have a changing station, diapers and extra clothes on both levels of the house. If you bottlefeed, have your partner prepare the nighttime bottle so that you don't have to make the extra trip down to the kitchen. Laundry is another consideration since many washer/dryer combinations are located in the basement of the house and most new mothers find themselves doing at least one load of baby clothes a day. Here's another area where your partner can be a help in the first few weeks, by taking over the laundry detail completely. Second, don't lift anything heavier than the baby. The baby may feel like a ton of bricks during the first few weeks after surgery, so you're unlikely to try to pick up anything else.

Third, don't drive the car. For the first two or three weeks, you should avoid driving a car. Many women wonder what could be the problem with driving. After all, with power steering and power brakes, it takes very little effort to come and go. However, in an emergency you might have to make a sudden move or push hard on the brake—difficult moves with a sore incision. Because your response in an emergency may be compromised, your doctor will ask you to hang up your keys until your recovery is well under way.

Of course, you can ride in the passenger seat, but don't let your sore abdomen keep you from securing yourself in your safety belt. Place a pillow or soft towel over your incision to cushion it from the pressure of the belt. You also don't need to tighten the belt to the point that it's uncomfortable.

SHOWERING AND BATHING   Whether you deliver vaginally or by Cesarean, you shouldn't take baths for the first couple of weeks while you have heavy lochia. The blood from the lochia is a very good medium for bacteria. Thus, while the lochia is heavy, you have a greater chance of having an infection develop and move up into your uterus. The water in which you bathe would be full of bacteria, which could enter the vagina and eventually the uterus. Showers offer less opportunity for infection to develop.

BREAST CHANGES

If you decided to bottlefeed, you'll probably go through a few days when your breasts are engorged at the onset of milk production. However, after milk production has been discouraged, your breasts will begin to return to their prepregnancy state. Some women feel that the shape of their breasts is exactly like it was before they became pregnant. Most women, however, notice a size and/or shape change.

Many women return to their original cup size, but some find that their breasts are actually smaller and fit better into a smaller cup size, or at least into a different style of bra. Few women who return to their normal weight find that their increase in cup size is permanent.

Your breasts' shape may be different depending on a number of factors, such as how elastic your skin is and how great your size increase was during pregnancy. If your breasts increased in size greatly—say, from an "A" cup to a "D"—the skin might not shrink all the way back to give your breasts the firm uplifted shape they had before pregnancy. Your breasts may appear slightly more pendulous and feel looser because of the excess skin. The tone of your breast skin probably will improve over the next few months, giving your breasts a firmer feel and appearance. However, they will not, in all likelihood, return to their prepregnancy firmness.

The aureola also may remain darker and larger in comparison with the rest of your breast than before you were pregnant, and you may notice red, spidery, or silvery stretch marks on the skin.

Many of you may be uncomfortable or even embarrassed by these vestigial reminders of your pregnancy. You might always be comparing your postpartum breasts negatively to your "virgin" breasts. The changes in size and shape may have been so dramatic in such a short period of time that you find it difficult to avoid making such comparisons.

Be reassured, however, that you'll become used to your new shape just as you became used to the shape of your breasts when they first developed. In fact, you can use the memory of that adjustment to help you make this one. Try to remember how you felt about your budding breasts, how you worried about the shape they'd take, how you compared them with those you didn't like and those you liked more. Eventually, you probably came to like or at least feel comfortable with your own shape then, just as you'll eventually come to feel comfortable with your new shape now.

If you are nursing your baby, your breasts will become a little fuller after your milk comes in. The changes in breasts during lactation are described fully in Chapter 5, "Breastfeeding,"

EXERCISE

As mentioned earlier, you'll be advised against strenuous exercise in these early weeks until your body has healed after delivery. Most mothers haven't the energy for any lengthy physical exertion anyway, so this prohibition is a welcome one.

It is important to get some gentle exercise in the first six weeks postpartum, however. You do want to encourage circulation and begin toning up muscles stretched out of shape during pregnancy. The new mother certainly can and should continue the exercise regimen she received in the hospital and add a daily walk to those gentle stretching and tightening exercises.

Regular exercise classes probably will be too demanding and even potentially harmful during your first six weeks postpartum. For example, you have to be wary of some popular exercises for tightening the abdomen, like leg lifts and sit ups. They put too much strain on the abdominal wall muscles which often have separated to accommodate the growing fetus. These muscles will realign naturally during the first six weeks postpartum, after which the mother can return to her normal exercise regimen. (See illustration p. 181)

The first six weeks of motherhood probably is not a realistic time to join a health club or commit yourself to exercise classes. You really need these first few weeks to work out some kind of mothering routine with your new baby. You need to find out when you have the most energy during the day, when your baby usually takes his or her naps, what the best times are for walks, and where the new mothers in your neighborhood congregate. Plugging into the mothering network in your neighborhood and meeting the needs of your infant will take up just about all of your energy for a day in the first few weeks of mothering.

Once your life falls more into place and you can see where you regularly have a free half hour, ask the other new mothers you meet about their fitness programs. Are there any good postpartum programs in your area? Which of the exercise books, records, and tapes for postpartum women are the most popular? You might want to stop by and watch a couple of the exercise classes given closest to you, or thumb through the recommended exercise books so that you'll have an idea of what kind of program you want to start once the first six weeks are up.

For women who have had Cesarean births, the restrictions on joining an exercise program may be in effect longer than the first six weeks. However, most recuperating C-section mothers won't feel comfortable enough to return to a rigorous exercise routine before the restrictions are lifted in any case. Except in unusual circumstances, restrictions on physical exertion don't go past two or three months.

BODY SHAPE

No matter what your weight is, you'll probably find that you're more comfortable in maternity clothes than any kind of regular clothes during these six weeks. If you have the courage to do some clothes shopping, you may find that you really don't fit into any regular size. Your waist is nonexistent and your belly still protrudes somewhat. That's normal for this time period.

After two weeks, your uterus will have contracted to the point that it can't be felt in the abdomen, but it will not reach its original size until the full six weeks have passed. Even after the uterus is back to its original size, however, your abdominal muscles will still be flaccid and protrude. It takes several months and a good exercise regimen to begin to get back muscle tone in the abdomen. During that time, you'll probably find that you don't fit into your old clothes regardless of your weight.

THE SIX-WEEK CHECKUP

Standard medical procedure calls for a follow-up visit at your obstetrician's or midwife's office six weeks after you deliver, although doctors' schedules for this visit do vary. Your doctor will check your general physical condition—listen to your heart, take your blood pressure, and check your weight. He or she also will do a breast examination to check for any suspicious lumps. If you are nursing, your nipples will be checked for soreness, cracks, or blisters. Mothers who delivered by Cesarean section will have their abdominal incisions examined to make sure that the tissue has healed properly. The muscles of the abdomen also will be checked to make sure that the abdominal wall is no longer separated, as it often is during pregnancy.

The doctor also will check your genitalia and, for women who had an episiotomy, the perineum to make sure that the incision there has healed.

The internal part of the examination may be somewhat uncomfortable for women who had an epiosotomy. Sometimes the scar tissue is still sensitive and lacks the elasticity of regular tissue. Stretching the tissue with the speculum (the instrument inserted and opened in the vagina to allow access to the cervix) may cause discomfort. However, the discomfort can be minimized by relaxing your muscles and taking a few deep breaths during the examination. Also ask the doctor to make sure that the speculum is well lubricated before it is inserted.

Nursing mothers also might notice some discomfort. Because of the low level of estrogen produced while a woman nurses, the vagina usually lacks elasticity and lubrication. As a result, the insertion and opening of the speculum can be more uncomfortable than normal. Here, too, muscle relaxation, deep breathing, and adequate lubrication on the speculum can make the examination easier to handle.

During the internal exam, your doctor will check the cervix to make sure that it shows no sign of tearing from the birth. He or she also will check the vaginal wall for signs of trauma from the birth. The size and position of your uterus will be determined to make sure that the involution process is completed and the uterus has returned to its normal position in your body. If there is any flow of lochia, that also will be examined to make sure that the color and odor are normal.

Most six-weeks exams are routine and normal. In the unusual case where problems are discovered, they usually fall into two categories: (1) retained products of conception (e.g. placental tissue) in the uterus, causing excess bleeding; or (2) failure of the uterus to involute to normal size, also causing excess bleeding.

If the uterus has not involuted, a drug that causes uterine contractions, such as pitocin, will be administered to stimulate involution. If the uterus has involuted but products of conception remain in the uterus, a D and C (dilation and curettage) will be performed to clean out the uterus. For the D and C, the practitioners will dilate your cervix and then use a spoon-shaped instrument to scrape clean your uterine lining.

At the end of your postpartum exam, your doctor will ask you if you plan to use contraceptives and discuss the various methods available (see "Contraceptives," p. 158).

Following your physical exam, your doctor might ask how you felt about the birth and how you are coping with motherhood. If you feel as if your case is being wrapped up and filed away, you're probably right. Assuming that your physical condition is normal, involution is complete, your abdominal muscles have rejoined, and any tears or incisions have healed, your doctor will declare that you have recovered from pregnancy and childbirth, shake your hand, and send you on your way with the advice to return to your normal semi annual schedule of gynecological examinations.

This is not entirely inappropriate. You probably don't need any more medical attention. However, most new mothers feel anything but fully recovered after six weeks. They're still tired, overweight, out of shape, and sore where incisions were stitched up. When their doctors declare them essentially recovered, most new mothers begin to wonder if they're going to stay that way forever. They also wonder who they'll be able to call when they have problems with breastfeeding, sex, weight loss, and fatigue, as most new mothers do. It's frightening for new mothers to be on their own suddenly after almost a year of continuous medical monitoring. And just for that reason it's important that you feel comfortable calling your doctor or the office nurse with your questions until you feel more confident. When your doctor shakes your hand, congratulates you, and says goodbye, mention that you'd like to feel free to call if you have any further questions. Most often, you'll be encouraged to do so.

LAURIE

Claire was a good nursing baby. Very enthusiastic right from the start. But I understand now how women get discouraged if they have problems. Nursing is not as wonderful as it's chalked up to be. I am glad I'm doing it and I would do it again, but I didn't find it to be as fulfilling an experience as I was led to believe it would be.

HEATHER

I had a four-month leave of absence from work, so I had a lot of time to be with Tucker and to nurse him. Before I had him, I felt that nursing for four months would be plenty. I had planned on weaning him so that I would be sure to fit back into my prepregnancy office clothes. I was visiting my mother just before I was to go back to work. She was helping me wean him. I was all bound up and uncomfortable, and Tucker wasn't really happy with the bottle. He wasn't as unhappy as I was though. There I was with my aching bound breasts unable to nurse him when he cried to eat. I would literally sob through the whole bottlefeeding session. At the end of three days, I woke up to feed him in the morning. He was fussing and I was fiddling around with a bottle. Finally I just had had enough. I decided to hell with my wardrobe, took off the binding, and nursed him. I went back to work one size larger and immeasurably happier.

5
BREASTFEEDING

Breastfeeding can in some ways be compared to lovemaking. At first you have the apparatus and you have a textbook notion of what to do with it, but the early encounters often don't live up to your expectations. It's not until you acquire a skill that either of these innate abilities become satisfying experiences. So it is that the first six weeks of nursing can be alternately frustrating, satisfying, convenient, inconvenient, painful, and soothing.

It is during this time that the greatest number of mothers who intended to nurse give up because of a variety of problems for which they were unprepared and for which they received inadequate support and guidance. New mothers need to understand that a successful nursing technique suitable both to you and your baby takes time to develop. The trial-and-error period is in the first month or two, when you discover what your baby's nursing style is as compared to what your nursing capacity is. Since feeding is such a large part of newborn care, the early setbacks in nursing can seem overwhelming. When you have sore nipples the first three weeks, and plugged ducts the next two, compounded by embarrassing leaking between feedings, you might begin to feel that you're just not cut out for nursing and turn to the bottle. If you do so, however, you've put yourself through the difficult part of nursing without ever enjoying the pleasures of breastfeeding. Most women find after the first six weeks to two months that suddenly the nursing routine falls into place. The baby naturally develops a three- or four-hour schedule, milk production stabilizes, a few tricks for encouraging the let-down reflex and unblocking plugged ducts are learned, and mother and baby finally can relax and enjoy these intimate minutes together.

There's a deep satisfaction in knowing that your nourishment is the source of your baby's development from a relatively scrawny newborn to a round-faced, stout-legged, energetic three- or six-month-old. Any mother who goes through the first six or eight difficult weeks of nursing shouldn't miss out on this sense of accomplishment. Many mothers only need an understanding of the problems they're having and some encouragement to work out solutions in order to develop a satisfying breastfeeding technique. I hope that the following overview of the body's milk-producing mechanisms, common problems that arise within them, and solutions to try will give you the information you need to make these first weeks of nursing go more smoothly.

CHANGES IN THE BREASTS

During pregnancy, the main milk duct system (mammary glands), present in your body since birth, branches out, undergoing rapid and extensive development in preparation for milk production. Each of these branched ducts empties into a milk pool, which feeds into one nipple opening. In the later stages of pregnancy, milk sacs (alveoli) develop off each duct. The milk is actually produced in the alveoli and then carried through the ducts to the milk pools. Colostrum, the clear, yellowish fluid produced before true milk, may occasionally be discharged from your nipples once the milk sacs are present. Thus, by the time you deliver your baby, your milk-producing capacity is fully established and ready for the hormonal signal to begin working. As mentioned earlier, this signal is given as soon as you deliver the placenta, when the hormone prolactin is released into your system, initiating milk production.

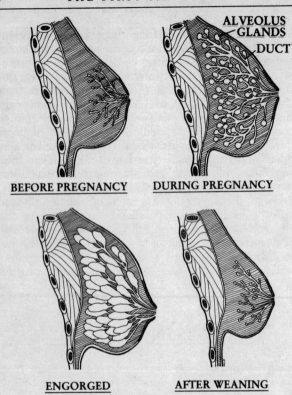

BEFORE PREGNANCY · **DURING PREGNANCY**

ALVEOLUS
GLANDS
DUCT

ENGORGED · **AFTER WEANING**

BREAST SIZE

Nursing mothers notice that their breasts become fuller when their milk production begins. The size of the breast is in no way related to milk supply. All women have about the same amount of mammary gland tissue. The variation in breast size from one woman to the next is due to the fat padding the milk-producing glands. Nursing mothers who have more fatty tissue in their breasts will be larger than mothers who have less fatty tissue. How much fatty tissue develops in your breasts is genetically controlled to a great extent, so every woman's increase in breast size during lactation is unique.

Because the amount of fatty tissue collection in the breast is individual, it's difficult to predict just how much bigger your breasts will be after you start to nurse. You're better off waiting until your milk comes in before buying a full supply of nursing bras. However, two nursing bras fitted generously will be useful in the hospital and for the first few days at home, until you're feeling strong enough to go out for a shopping expedition. Make sure that your bras are soft and comfortable and are not lined with plastic. The plastic, meant to prevent milk leakage from coming through the bra, holds in moisture, which can aggravate nipple soreness (See "Leaking," p. 109).

Your best bet is to buy two or three bras initially and then wait to fill out your supply until your milk supply is established (meaning that milk production is at peak efficiency), in a month or two. You may notice that your breasts actually get smaller, although you're making *more* milk at this point to meet the greater demands of your growing infant. The decrease in size is a result of the efficiency of your milk production. The additional blood supply that swelled your breasts during the onset of lactation is no longer needed. Also, your breasts are falling into a production schedule where they produce just as much milk as you need when you need it according to your baby's demands.

BREAST ENGORGEMENT

For some women, the initial engorgement (painful swelling) of the breasts that accompanies the onset of milk production recurs before feedings for a few weeks until the milk supply is established, or when there's a longer than usual period between nursings. The engorgement will be quickly relieved by putting the baby to breast—a most satisfactory solution for mother and baby. However, the breast may become so full that the nipple and aureola are hard for your newborn to take in his or her mouth. Gentle hand or pump expression of a few drops of milk can soften the nipple enough for the baby to be able to position him or herself properly on the aureola (see "Milk Expression," p. 104)

Engorgement usually decreases gradually as your body adjusts to the milk production process. You may still feel a fullness before a regular nursing time, but the painful swelling won't persist.

LET-DOWN REFLEX

When you begin to nurse your newborn, the sucking triggers the release of a the hormone oxytocin. Oxytocin causes the milk-producing alveoli and the milk ducts to contract, sending the milk into the pools located beneath the aureola and out through the nipple sinuses. This is the let-down reflex. If your newborn's mouth is correctly positioned over the nipple and the aureola, his or her jawing actions and sucking also will squeeze the milk pools and help draw the milk out through the nipple.

The let-down reflex is commonly associated with a tingling or drawing sensation in the breasts. However, not every woman feels a clear sensation when her milk lets down. Those who don't often worry that their milk is not being made available to their newborns.

If you don't sense your milk letting down, you can assuage anxieties about your nursing ability in a number of ways.

- Watch your newborn's behavior during feeding. Does he or she seem content nursing and satisfied after each feeding? A baby who is frustrated at the breast for lack of milk will let you know it in no uncertain terms.
- Check diapers. A baby who wets sixteen to twenty diapers a day is adequately fed.
- Keep track of weight gain. Another indicator of successful nursing is weight gain, which is carefully monitored by the pediatrician during the first months of life.
- Express your milk. If outward signs of successful breastfeeding don't satisfy you, try expressing some

milk just before you nurse to see if your milk is indeed flowing despite your lack of sensation during let-down (see "Milk Expression," p. 104).

MILK SUPPLY

Your milk production is based on a supply and demand schedule. If you don't nurse your baby at all and there is no demand for the milk, milk production will stop. If you nurse your baby every three hours, you'll produce enough milk to feed your baby every three hours. If your baby needs a greater supply of milk and nurses more frequently for a day or so, your milk supply will increase to meet his or her greater needs.

However, this supply and demand system takes a few weeks to function efficiently, for several reasons. Initially, your newborn's nursing habits may not be regular. He or she may suck heartily on one side and nod off on the other. The newborn's sucking ability also may take time to become efficient. At the same time, your body also is trying to become efficient at producing milk. Adequate circulating levels of prolactin and oxytocin have to be established to stimulate milk production and facilitate let-down. The combination of your baby's erratic sucking habits and your fluctuating hormone levels in the first few weeks may lead to an uneven milk supply. But once you and your baby become more accustomed to the nursing routine, your milk supply will become established. The most common indication is that you don't have to think about nursing anymore. Your let-down reflex is reliable, and you can count on your baby to empty both breasts efficiently.

WHAT TO WEAR

What is the best cover for a nursing mother? That question really has to be answered by the individual woman. A T-shirt works best for many small- to medium-breasted women, but large-breasted women may find that it doesn't provide adequate cover. They might prefer a looser shirt that gives them more fabric to drape.

One rule of thumb does prevail, however, and that is to use shirts that lift up rather than dresses that must be unbuttoned and pulled aside. The shirts always give you more convenient cover. In cooler weather, some nursing mothers find that shawls and ponchos are helpful for modest breastfeeding also.

MILK EXPRESSION

Many women find milk expression difficult. However, as with other nursing problems, the difficulty often is due to a lack of information and preparation rather than an inability to express milk.

Milk expression is an important part of breastfeeding in that it allows the nursing mother to have more free time than just the couple of hours between feedings without compromising her milk supply or becoming engorged and uncomfortable. Furthermore, if the expressed milk is frozen or stored in the refrigerator overnight, it can be used in a substitute bottle so that the baby drinks mother's milk rather than formula even when mom's away from home. Milk expression, in other words, gives the nursing mother some of the freedom and convenience of bottle-feeding.

The problems with milk expression are twofold. First, many women find manual expression a difficult skill to acquire but then can't find a breast pump that works satisfactorily either. Second, most mothers find that their let-down reflex doesn't work efficiently when they are expressing milk. Part of the problem may have to do with the feeling of being exposed if you're expressing milk in a public place. In general, our society is not friendly toward nursing mothers. Many nursing mothers find that the only place they can express their milk when away from home is in a stall in the ladies' room, not an environment conducive to relaxation. Part of the problem also may have to do with the lack of regular let-down cues, such as hearing your baby cry, picking him or her up, and settling into your normal nursing position. These problems can be solved once they are understood.

First, if you want to get comfortable with expressing your milk, don't wait until you're at a friend's house or back at your office to try it. Make your first effort at home, where you're most comfortable. You might try it a few times just before you pick your baby up to nurse. Before you start, make sure you use the same relaxation tricks you might use when nursing your baby and your let-down hesitates. Get a glass of water or juice. Sit down. Take a deep breath and let it out slowly. Close your eyes and relax for a moment. You might find that stroking your breasts toward your nipples for a few moments also encourages let-down. You might even imagine hearing your baby stirring from a nap and starting to fuss from hunger. Once you're relaxed and maybe even beginning to feel the initial tingle of let-down, try to express some milk either with your hand or with a pump.

Most women find that they are more successful expressing milk at one time during the day than another. If you are not able to express much milk at one time, don't assume you won't meet with success. Try taking some milk at varying times until you find those that are best for you.

Even if you use a pump for convenience most of the time, you should understand how to express milk with your hands in case you need to do so when a pump is unavailable. Keep in mind while you try this that you're trying to imitate as best you can the action of the baby's jaws on your nipple and aureola. You're trying to draw out the milk from the pools beneath the aureola. Therefore, the pressure should be on the aureola, not on your nipple. To begin expressing milk, place a cup under one nipple. Then, take hold of the nipple by placing the thumb on top of the aureola and the fingers below. Press down and *back* on the outer edge of the aureola to express the milk out. You may not see any milk for a few seconds until your milk lets down, then you will see a fine spray coming out of the nipple when you apply the down-and-

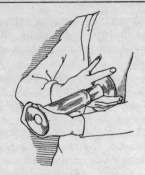

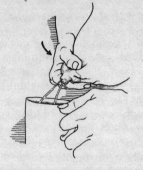

PUMP EXPRESSION WITH
PORTABLE PUMP

MANUAL MILK EXPRESSION
(DOWN-AND BACK MOTION)

back pressure. Continue reapplying the pressure until the milk flow stops. Then, repeat on the other side.

If hand expression works well for you, you may not need or want to use a pump. However, for many women a good pump makes expressing milk easier. Most professionals and mothers agree that there's only one efficient manual pump, the Kaneson or Marshall pump, which is made of a plastic tube fitted within a plastic sleeve that has an opening for the nipple on the top. By pulling on the outer plastic tube, you draw out the milk from the breast. When you're finished expressing milk, the inner sleeve can be removed and the outer tube can be used either as a bottle (the pump comes with cover and nipple to fit) or a storage container.

If you've tried the bulb-and-horn-type pump and had little success expressing milk, as is frequently the case, give yourself another chance with the Kaneson pump. Though not as portable as a hand pump, a battery-operated may be quicker and easier to use for some mothers who express milk most often at home.

Once you've become experienced with hand or pump expression, you may find it easier to let-down when you're out of the house—even if you have to express milk in the lavatory. The key is to make yourself comfortable and relaxed.

Expressed milk can be frozen and later defrosted in the refrigerator or under lukewarm water or it can be refrigerated if you're going to use it within a few hours. If you express milk away from home you either can throw it out or, if you have access to a refrigerator, keep it chilled until you're ready to go home. A particularly convenient container for expressed milk is a Playtex Nurser refill bag. The bag—which comes sterilized—can be stretched over the nurser sleeve, filled with milk from the pump, then sealed with a flexible twist, and frozen in the freezer until you need the milk. When you want to use the milk, you thaw it out in the refrigerator and simply slip the refill back over the nurser sleeve.

COMMON NURSING PROBLEMS

COPING WITH UNRELIABLE LET-DOWN

The let-down reflex is indeed a reflex in that it is automatic and outside of your control, but it is a temperamental one. Let-down is controlled by the pituitary gland, which is in turn controlled by the hypothalamus, a part of the brain referred to as the seat of emotions. The hypothalamus translates our feelings into physiological reactions by controlling the secretion of hormones from the body's glands. Because the let-down reflex is indirectly controlled by the hypothalamus, it is strongly influenced by our psychological state. Unlike your knee-jerk reflex, which can be elicited at any moment by a tap in the right place, let-down can be elusive when you most need it, or effusive when you least expect it. You may feel the tingling or drawing sensation when *any* baby cries within earshot while you're out of the house, but when you get home you have to make a concerted effort to relax before your milk lets down.

Relaxation is critical to successful nursing. If you're particularly tired or anxious—as many new mothers are in the first few weeks after birth—your let-down reflex might fail to function at all. This, of course, will probably make you even more panicky. You might feel that you're going to starve your newborn. The baby will respond, too, crying and fussing out of hunger and in response to your tension. Then, of course, you get more upset as does your baby, and a frustrating cycle begins. If the cycle continues for even a couple of days, you may get the impression that you don't have enough milk to feed your baby, or that your let-down reflex isn't sufficient. In this case, your physiological capacity is probably not the source of the problem. Instead, your anxiety is impeding the normal production and let-down of milk.

To stop the cycle, try one or more of the following measures to help you relax and encourage your milk to let down:

- Establish a routine for nursing that takes you away from whatever you are doing. Some women have a favorite chair they settle into. Others keep the nursing chair in the baby's room so they can get away from whatever other concerns are around them and concentrate on the baby.
- When you sit down to nurse, have a tall glass of liquid nearby. Drink heartily, take a deep breath, and then start to nurse.
- Sometimes a glass of beer or wine drunk a few minutes before a feeding session can relieve the mother of a day's tension before she starts to nurse.
- If you're having persistent problems with your let-down reflex, talk to your pediatrician about giving you an oxytocin inhaler to help your let-down reflex get established.
- One rule of thumb that most nursing mothers learn is to consciously avoid making the feedings an anxiety-provoking event. Once breastfeeding becomes a source of anxiety for mother and baby, it is almost doomed to fail if the anxiety is not somehow resolved. When a feeding isn't going smoothly, rather than try ever more intently to make the breastfeeding work, you would do better to lean back in the chair, close your eyes, take a deep breath, and relax. Once you are calm again, you can try the nursing from the start. Remember that nursing should be a nurturing, emotionally satisfying experience, not a battle between mother and infant.

•Call a friend who is nursing or the La Leche League for support. Maybe your confidante will have had a similar problem and be able to share her solution. You'll probably find that your situation is a common one, which will make you feel more at ease and less insecure about your nursing ability.

As with any other part of nursing, the let-down reflex becomes more dependable as you become more accustomed to your nursing routine. At first, you may find that it takes a couple of minutes of sucking before your milk lets down, but as the weeks go by you'll find your milk available within seconds of putting the baby to the breast.

LEAKING   A lot has been mentioned here about trouble with the let-down reflex, meaning that it doesn't function for some reason and milk won't flow. However, many mothers experience another kind of let-down problem—leaking milk between feedings. Milk leaking occurs when the let-down reflex is triggered for some reason at an inappropriate moment, like during dinner at a restaurant, in the supermarket, or at the office. After the familiar tingling of the reflex, the mother will begin to notice that her bra and shirt are damp from milk leaking from her breasts. The trigger for the reflex can be anything from the thought of the mother's baby to the sound of another baby to the passing of a scheduled nursing time.

Not every nursing mother has a problem with leaking, and some mothers only have a problem during the early weeks. But a number of women leak between feedings from the time they start to nurse to the time they wean. Nothing can be done to stop the reflex, but the leaking can be managed in the following ways:

•Whenever you feel the let-down reflex start when you don't want to nurse, press the heels of your hands or your forearms firmly against your breasts. Sometimes this stops the reflex.
•Make sure that you wear nursing pads in your bra to

absorb leaks. You can use either disposable pads or washable cotton ones. When you're going to be out for several hours, take an extra supply of pads with you so that you can change them if they get damp. Leaving damp pads in place will irritate the nipples.

•If you're going to be away from home past the time you normally nurse, try to get to a private area when the feeding would usually take place and express a little milk. This might prevent the let-down later on as the breasts become engorged.

•Wear blouses, shirts, or dresses with light prints. If you do leak milk, these patterns and colors will not reveal the wetness as would dark solid colors.

MILK SUPPLY PROBLEMS   Some of the most common problems with an inadequate milk supply have less to do with biological inadequacies in the new mother than they do with inadequate diet, rest, encouragement, and information. A mother who is chronically exhausted because she's trying to fit in too many activities into her day and who is cutting back on her nutrition in an effort to lose weight is not giving her body a chance to produce an adequate supply of milk. Also, many women don't drink enough to restore the body fluid lost to breast milk manufacture. Nursing mothers need to drink two to three quarts of fluid a day (see Chapter 7).

As important as rest and diet, however, is encouragement and information. If you are having normal problems with let-down and supply in the early weeks of nursing, you need the support of your pediatrician and perhaps another nursing mother to help you get past these hurdles. If your pediatrician is too quick to tell you that you can't provide enough nutrition for your newborn, or if you are surrounded by friends and relatives who discourage breastfeeding at the slightest sign of a problem, you'll probably lose your confidence before you and your baby have had a chance to get settled in a nursing routine.

When you interview pediatricians either before or just after birth, make sure you ask a question about their view on nursing. Find out what percentage of the mothers in the practice nurse their children and for how long. Find out who in the office is the nursing maven—the person to contact with your uncertainties and problems. You need a practitioner who is going to help you handle any difficulties that arise during the early weeks of nursing and who also can dispel any inaccurate advice you might get from friends and relatives who mean well but actually sabotage your efforts to breastfeed.

In a very few cases, however, a mother does produce too little or too *much* milk. In the former case, she may work out a system with the pediatrician where the baby is breastfed but also receives a supplementary bottle when necessary. In the latter case, the mother can express a little milk before each feeding to make the flow of milk more manageable for the baby.

MILK QUALITY Human milk quality generally doesn't vary much. Even if you're undernourished, your body will cannibalize its own nutrients to make milk of adequate quality for your baby. Unlike milk supply and the let-down reflex, milk quality is one part of breastfeeding that the new mother can do little to influence. However, in order to make sure that her body and the baby are being nourished adequately, she should make sure that she eats a healthy diet and adds about 500 calories to her daily diet (see Chapter 7).

FATIGUE New mothers are often tired in the first six weeks after birth just from the postpartum recovery combined with the new responsibilities of motherhood. However, some women feel that nursing saps their energy as well. If you find that breastfeeding has a draining effect, just make sure you put aside enough time for adequate rest. Remember that each mother responds differently to early motherhood and nursing. Try not to measure yourself by other mothers' responses. If you know someone who is full of energy to "get things accomplished" between feedings while you drop into bed for naps, don't feel guilty about your need for rest. The difference in energy just reflects differences in the way your body copes with the demands of nursing.

SORE NIPPLES Before you had your baby, you probably got lots of advice about preparing your nipples for nursing—toughening them up. You were supposed to rub them with a towel after showers, roll them between your fingers, and go braless to allow the nipples to rub against the cloth of your shirt or dress. Unfortunately, if you're fair-skinned, you probably still are going to experience some nipple soreness. Much will depend on your baby's nursing style; voracious suckers cause more sore nipples than do gentle suckers. Once your nipples are sore, the first few seconds of nursing can be hard to face. However, when your milk has let-down, the soreness should fade.

There are several avenues to take to minimize soreness and help desensitize nipples:

- Make sure that your baby is taking the whole aureola into his or her mouth, not just the nipple. Nipple sucking is a sure way to sore nipples and doesn't help the baby draw out milk from the milk pools beneath the aureola.
- Don't use soaps or alcohol to clean your nipples before feeding the baby. A plain water rinse during your daily bath is all that's needed to keep your nipples clean. All you accomplish by using harsh soaps or alcohol on your nipples is to wash away the natural lubrication provided by special oil glands called Montgomery's glands. These glands look like raised bumps or pimples on your aureolas. The oil they secrete lubricates and protects your nipples while you're breastfeeding.
- Try using a cream such as lanolin (if you're not allergic to wool), masse cream, or A&D ointment on your breasts after you shower and after feedings. These creams will keep the nipples' skin soft and may help prevent drying and cracking. If you do use a

INCORRECT POSITION   CORRECT POSITION
OF MOUTH ON NIPPLE   OF MOUTH ON NIPPLE
(ONLY NIPPLE TAKEN)   (AUREOLA AND NIPPLE TAKEN)

cream, rinse your nipples with water before nursing
the baby.

•Between feedings leave the cup flaps of your nursing
bra down to expose your nipples to the air as often as
possible. You want the nipples to be as dry as possible between feedings.

•Exposing your nipples to sunlight or an incandescent
lamp for a few minutes also can contribute to diminishing soreness.

•Since one nipple usually is sorer than the other, try
nursing on the *less* sore side first so that that side
takes the brunt of the baby's first hard sucking. After
your newborn is partially satiated, he or she will
suck more gently on the sore nipple.

•Your baby also will suck less vigorously if you stimulate your breasts before nursing to get the milk
flowing. The baby won't need to nurse as hard to
initiate the let-down reflex. Manual expression or a
breast pump can elicit the letdown reflex just before
you nurse (see "Milk Expression," p. 104).

•Changing nursing positions also can take the pressure
off the sore area of the nipple. If you usually nurse
sitting up, try nursing lying on your side. If you
normally cradle the baby during feedings, try the
football hold (see illustration).

**TRADITIONAL
SITTING POSITION**

FOOTBALL HOLD POSITION

RECLINING POSITION

- Use your breathing techniques to get through the first few seconds of sucking.
- Try taking two aspirin or aspirin-free pain relievers a half hour before nursing. The pain reliever might minimize the discomfort you feel.
- If soreness persists for several weeks, check with

NIPPLE GUARD

your pediatrician to see if your baby has thrush, a mouth infection that can lead to nipple soreness.

If these steps don't help you get over the hurdle of sore nipples, ask your pediatrician about obtaining and using nipple guards. The guards are rubber shields that fit over your nipple and allow the baby to nurse without sucking harshly on the sore area. The guards, however, may not allow enough stimulation of the nipple over a long period of time to build up your supply of milk. They are only a temporary measure for a day or so to give your sore nipple a rest. Nipple guards are frowned upon by some of the more radical proponents of breastfeeding, but if they help you attain your goal of successfully nursing your child, then they are working for you.

CRACKED AND/OR BLEEDING NIPPLES

If your nipples become so irritated that they begin to crack and bleed, you may find it too painful to nurse for a day or two. This doesn't mean that you have to stop nursing. Instead, you can give your baby a bottle for several feedings and use a hand breast pump every three hours to express milk and keep up your production. The pump won't exert the pressure on your nipple that sucking would, so it won't cause the discomfort of breastfeeding. Usually, twelve hours on the pump will give you enough of a respite to begin nursing again, although you still will experience some discomfort at first.

When your nipples have healed a bit, try putting the baby to breast after you've gotten the milk flowing by manual or pump expression. Just nurse for the minimum five minutes on each side at first. Most babies can drain a

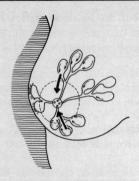

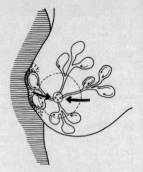

UP-AND-DOWN JAW
ACTION DRAWS MILK
UNEVENLY FROM
DUCTS. PARTIALLY
EMPTIED DUCTS MAY
BECOME CLOGGED
AND INFLAMED.

A CHANGE IN
NURSING POSITION
ENCOURAGES
DRAINING OF
CLOGGED DUCT,
RELIEVING
INFLAMMATION.

breast in the first five minutes of nursing once they're efficient nursers, so you won't be depriving your child of any nourishment. He or she may have sucking needs that go unmet, though, and a pacifier might be good to have on hand in that event. Try dipping it in sugar water or some expressed breast milk if the taste of the rubber or plastic makes your baby refuse it at first.

BLOCKED DUCTS   The bane of many new nursing mothers, blocked milk ducts, develop when accumulated milk in a duct cannot pass through the nipple. The blocked duct usually feels like a sore, hot lump that may be slightly reddened from the irritation.

Causes for blocked nipples vary. They can occur if dried milk clogs a nipple sinus so that milk can't flow through it. This is one reason for washing off your nipples with water before nursing. Sometimes a bra fitted too tightly can be the cause of a clogged duct. If you've grown out of your nursing bras, don't try to squeeze into them. The investment in a well-fitted bra is important for successful breastfeeding.

Blocked ducts also can occur if the let-down reflex is functioning irregularly during the first few weeks of nursing. This can result in an accumulation of milk in a duct and consequent irritation.

In addition, they are frequently caused when a mother stays with a favored nursing position too long. The jaw action of the baby is up and down, so the sinuses on only two sides of the nipples are being drawn on in any one position. Some of the milk ducts are not drained. This won't lead to a problem if the baby is nursed in different positions so that all the milk ducts are drained regularly. However, if a mother nurses in only one position for an extended period of time, the undrained milk ducts may become congested and plugged.

If you have a plugged duct, you can try the following methods for clearing it. First, wash your nipples with water before nursing. Next, put hot compresses on the affected areas. A hot shower also may do the trick. Then, massage the affected area with pressure toward the nipple. Now you're ready to start the feeding. Start with the affected breast first so that the baby's early strong sucking action can work on and hopefully free the clogged duct. Your baby's sucking is one of the most effective means of freeing a plugged duct if you position him or her so that the up-and-down jaw action can exert the most pressure on the area with the plugged duct.

After you breastfeed, drain the affected breast as much as possible with a breast pump. You might also want to nurse more frequently for a longer period of time on the affected side.

MASTITIS OR BREAST INFECTIONS A breast infection can follow the formation of a plugged duct, in which case bacteria in the congested duct start the process. However, a plugged duct is not always a precursor to mastitis. You can get a breast infection also if bacteria in your baby's mouth, for instance, enters the breast through the nipple.

Signs of mastitus include engorgement of the breast, which will be hot and tender to the touch. The mother also is likely to feel headachy and feverish—almost as if she had a flu.

If you have these symptoms, get in touch with your obstetrician or midwife. Usually, you will be advised to *continue* nursing. Milk from the infected breast in most instances won't have an adverse effect on the baby, and frequent emptying of the breast will encourage recovery. Your practitioner may prescribe pain relievers and/or antibiotics, but will do so with your breastfeeding needs in mind.

Aside from calling the doctor, you should treat yourself as if you *have* got the flu. Go to bed. Soothe the breast with warm compresses and concentrate on getting well. Ignoring a breast infection won't make it go away but can lead to complications, the most common being a breast abscess.

BREAST ABSCESS   An abscess is a more severe breast infection, in which pus collects in one area of the breast around tissue already inflamed by infection. When an abscess forms it may be treated with antibiotics, or it may have to be lanced and drained. Until the infection is treated, you won't be able to nurse from the affected breast. However, you should drain the breast as frequently and fully as possible and throw away the milk. This will encourage recovery and also will keep your milk supply up so that you can continue nursing on both sides once the abscess is treated.

After the first six weeks or so, nursing will become second nature for most mothers. You might have an occasional let-down problem, plugged duct or bout of engorgement when your milk supply increases, but you'll know how to deal with these minor problems. After all, you'll be practicing how to nurse every two to three hours day and night! With that much practice, you can't help but become an expert.

MAGGIE

I'm nursing my second child now. I love it, but I find that nursing takes so much out of me. I remember how tired I always felt while I was nursing my firstborn. As soon as I weaned, I had a surge of energy. I could get up an hour earlier and go to sleep an hour later every day. That's one drawback to breastfeeding—the constant fatigue. Much as I enjoy it, I'll be happy to have my energy back.

MARIE

The odd thing about my first few months—waking up every two hours to feed Willie—was that I wasn't tired. I don't know what I was running on, but I had a lot of energy. I found this new aspect of mothering an infant so exciting, I guess, that I had a lot of energy. But the lack of sleep did catch up with me. When I weaned Willie, I found that I was exhausted all the time. I took naps, which I never do. I fell asleep while riding in the car, which I also never do. I couldn't get out of bed in the morning and couldn't wait to get into bed at night. This is the same woman who went out and bicycled for forty-five minutes every morning when she was still nursing every two to three hours.

6
FATIGUE

For most women, fatigue is inevitable in the first few weeks of motherhood. The most common reason given for this exhaustion is sleep interruption. While lack of restorative sleep is certainly a major cause of postpartum fatigue, other factors play a significant role also:

First, recovering from the tremendous exertion of labor and delivery requires physical rest that is difficult for most new mothers to find time for.

Second, some mothers come home slightly anemic (having a low red blood cell count) for the first few weeks following birth because of blood loss during birth. The anemia may be self-correcting and require no special medical treatment, or it may simply require taking an iron supplement for several months. New mothers who are slightly anemic will fatigue easily for three or so weeks until their bodies begin to restore the normal level of red blood cells.

Third, the postpartum woman's body is going through enormous changes during the first few weeks, ridding itself of excess fluids, returning the uterus to its normal size and place, and stabilizing the hormonal fluctuations that occur at birth. During this initial recovery process, you're likely to feel drained just as you would during any other recuperative process.

Finally, the initiation and maintenance of milk production is another demand on your physical resources that taps your limited energy stores and makes you feel more fatigued.

Because of all of these changes (and perhaps more if the delivery is complicated), the new mother has a very low reserve of energy when she comes home. However, her new baby will tax those low energy reserves unmercifully to get the food and attention he or she requires. Balancing the new mother's need for rest and the new baby's need for attention takes vigilant attention to priorities: your baby's health and your recuperation come first. Below, you'll find some insights into the common consequences of chronic fatigue, some suggestions for coping with it, and some warning signs of when it's getting the best of you.

REST WHEN THE BABY RESTS

You should live by this rule in the first few weeks. In order to nurture your newborn and recuperate at the same time, you need to sleep or rest when the baby sleeps and focus your energies on mothering when the baby's awake. Use disposable dinnerware and let the dust collect. Your house will survive a few weeks of minimal upkeep.

SLEEP DEPRIVATION

Even if you heed the above advice, you'll probably only get short two- to four-hour naps in the first months of motherhood. In a day, you might get seven or eight hours' sleep, but you're still likely to feel drained, exhausted, and edgy. Much of these feelings come from REM (rapid eye movement) sleep deprivation. REM sleep occurs cyclically throughout the night and is the part of the sleep cycle associated with dreams. The most intense dreaming activity takes place in the latter couple of hours in a seven- or eight-hour night's rest. REM sleep is necessary for our psychological and physical well-being. If your REM cycle is disrupted often enough, you'll build up a REM sleep deficit that often shows itself in feelings of exhaustion and lack of emotional resilience. You're also likely to notice feelings of near panic when the baby begins to cry just as you've slipped into the deep sleep cycle you need.

If you are nursing or bottlefeeding your newborn around the clock, you may only get two or three hours of sleep at one time. Some mothers seem to manage to get enough REM sleep in this fragmented kind of rest. Others, however, build up a greater and greater need for sleep as the weeks go by.

If you find that you are not getting any satisfying sleep, try alternating one night feeding with your partner so that each of you can get at least five or six hours of restorative sleep at night. If you are breastfeeding and are concerned about the missed nocturnal feedings disturbing your milk supply, try skipping a feeding every other night. You also can express your milk just before you go to bed to help build up your supply.

You might also try feeding the baby as close as possible to your bedtime. If you're nursing and you feed the baby an hour and a half or more before you go to bed, nurse him or her again just before you retire. The extra feeding might give you a little extra sleep.

Be reassured that most babies drop one night feeding by the time they're three months old, so you should be able to get five to six hours of sleep regularly by that time.

THE BABY'S CRY

Being awakened from a sound sleep several times a night is bad enough, but to be jolted awake by the piercing cry of your infant is truly a nerve-shattering experience.

Your baby's cry is meant to be a distress signal you can't ignore. The sound elicits not only an emotional response but a physical one as well. When your baby cries, your blood pressure surges, your breathing quickens, and you begin to perspire more. This is the same response you have to sudden loud noises, strange sounds in the house at night, or burning your hand on a hot pot. Physiologically, you're primed for an emergency.

While every mother has the urge to comfort her infant when she hears him or her crying, the intensity of that urge varies across a broad spectrum. Some women seem only mildly affected by the cries, unhurriedly rousing themselves to pick up the baby. Others rush to their babies to quiet the crying with a greater sense of urgency. And the mothers who are the most sensitive to their babies' cries feel an almost visceral shock which propels them out of bed to the infant's side in one leap.

None of these innate responses is better or worse than another. If you have a calmer response to your baby's cries than your friend does to hers, don't doubt your maternal instinct. As long as you're answering the cries, your mothering is as good as your friend's. The opposite is true also. If your instinct is to comfort your newborn the very instant he or she starts to whimper, don't be deterred by old wives' tales that you're spoiling your infant. Keep in mind that newborns can't be spoiled. They need all the attention they seem to want.

COLIC

If your exposure to your newborn's crying was only for a moment or two before a feeding or changing, crying wouldn't be an issue. However, most infants at some time between the ages of six weeks and three months go through daily crying fits when no amount of soothing, feeding, distraction, or changing can stop the howling. Many infants become inconsolable for two to three hours in the afternoon or evening during this period, so the crying fits are known as afternoon or evening colic. A small percentage of children, often labeled as colicky, cry for eighteen or more hours a day in these early months.

The first feeling you'll probably have when your baby starts to wail as if he or she were being tortured is to whisk him or her into your arms and rock, walk, pat, feed, burp, change, bathe, or bounce the discomfort away. When all of your best efforts fail, though, you're likely first to feel disappointed in yourself and then desperate to stop the crying. After all, the crying—especially at this intense pitch—is a physical distress signal to you. Being kept on edge with your blood pressure up and your heart pounding when you can't do anything to stop the crying is frustrating and exhausting.

What you can do for yourself to mitigate the emotional and physical drain of these periods of intense crying is to try and prepare for them if your baby is colicky in the afternoon or evening, or get away from them for a little while each day if your child is colicky most of the time.

If you know that the crying starts at about the same time each day, try to get a break from mothering for an hour or so to replenish your emotional stores before your baby's mood changes. If the crying goes on for several hours each night, try alternating shifts with your partner so that each of you gets a breather. Many partners tend to sit through these trying periods together as a sign of support. However, as the tension and frustration caused by the baby's wailing increase, the partners often take out their irritation on one another. Instead of being supportive, they often end up castigating each other for their inability to soothe the baby. Offering periodic relief from the crying is often a more effective support than sitting through the colicky period together.

If your baby is colicky around the clock, make sure that you get some relief so that you're not alone with your inconsolable child all day long. Many mothers of colicky children worry about leaving their wailing infants with sitters. They can barely suffer the aural onslaught, how could a stranger? If you're not comfortable with a sitter, have a friend or relative who feels confident about caring for your baby relieve you for an hour or two each day. Also, let your partner solo with the baby for a night or two a week so that you can get a block of time to enjoy a movie or dine out with some friends. Equally important is having some time away from the crying with your partner. Here again, if you're uncomfortable hiring a sitter, ask a friend to take over for an hour or two so you both can take a walk together or have a quick dinner.

DEPRESSION

For some new mothers, the first few weeks of adjusting to a newborn's needs go fairly smoothly. They don't seem as tired as they were told they would be. They don't mind letting the house go for a while. They just close the door on the mess and go to the park. These mothers have no trouble dozing while the baby sleeps. They also don't mind eating frozen dinners for a few weeks until some parenting routine is established, or letting their daily schedule fluctuate with the baby's. If they don't have a chance to shower and dress until 4 P.M., they don't care.

However, for other mothers the physical limitations and schedule irregularities make life irritating. The new mother can't go shopping because she can't carry the groceries. The necessities are all at home, but the right size plastic bag, a favorite kind of soup, or the right brand of juice and detergent might be missing. And the state of the house can take a dramatic turn for the worse. The meticulously neat woman looks up to find dust balls rolling across the bedroom floor, or innumerable pieces of cloth strewn about the house to catch the baby's burps and diaper leaks, or bottles and nipples and pacifiers and rattles stacked or dropped on every surface. After years of orderly living, suddenly there's chaos, and neither she nor her partner has the time or energy to do anything about it because the baby needs a bath or has evening colic or needs to be fed or has to be changed.

The combination of fatigue, household disorder, and the demands of a newborn all can consort to make this new mother weepy and anxious and depressed. Motherhood suddenly seems too overwhelming for one chronically exhausted person to handle everyday.

The kind of depression that sets in towards the end of the first six weeks of motherhood is not the same as the "baby blues" that you might have experienced for a few days just after birth. The "baby blues" are characterized by weepiness, changeable mood, anxiety, and resolution after a week or so. The depression that occurs at this time is more a reflection of chronic fatigue and emotional over-extension. The early signs of depression may be similar to the "baby blues," but a sense of entrapment and isolation, inability to sleep, poor appetite, and loss of motivation also develop.

Many women experience these feelings in the first three months of motherhood. Often they come and go over that period, depending on how much support the mother is getting at home, how isolated she is from her regular activities, and how much rest she is able to get.

In a fairly typical scenario, the partner saves up about two weeks' vacation to stay at home with the family for the first two weeks. After that, a relative or professional caregiver comes in for another two weeks. During this time the majority of well-wishers also make their visits. Then, at the end of the first month, the new mother often finds herself at home alone with a baby who is fussier than the day he or she was taken home, who requires feeding every two to four hours and rocking, bathing, and diapering in between, and who doesn't allow her more than three hours of sleep at a time. She finds it harder and harder to rekindle her feelings of elation at being a mother and begins to feel isolated, overwhelmed, and panicky at the loss of control over her life. She may feel great remorse at being cut off from her normal lifestyle—her work, her partner, her sexual self, and her friends—and long for the special attention and care she received during her pregnancy.

In most instances, these feelings persist for a week or two but then subside as the new mother's friends, relatives, and partner provide the support she needs to regain her equilibrium. A friend might sit for a few hours while the new parents go out to dinner once a week. A relative might contribute dinners for a week or two. The new mother might make arrangements to have more help at home. And the baby, too, will help in many instances, by sleeping a little longer between feedings and at night.

Support seems to be the primary means of resolving this form of mild depression. The sense of despair and isolation might recur several times during the first month or two of motherhood, but a good listener, some reliable childcare, and a few hours alone with a good friend or a partner can usually pull the new mother out of her depression.

> If the new mother doesn't have a support network to help her cope with her postpartum adjustment, or is prone to developing long lasting depression, she may become increasingly despondent until she is unable to care for herself or the new baby. Signs of this more serious, chronic depression include the following:
>
> - Basic tasks such as bathing, dressing, and feeding the infant, getting out of bed and dressed for the day, cooking, washing dishes, straightening the house, or shopping for necessities seem overwhelming and impossible to handle.
> - Immobilizing feelings of despair, isolation, anxiety and helplessness alternate with feelings of apathy and extreme fatigue.
> - Despite feeling tired all of the time, the depressed mother sleeps fitfully.
> - Loss of appetite.
>
> If you recognize these common signs of chronic depression in yourself, you need to see a health professional for help. Contact your midwife or obstetrician for guidance.

HELP AT HOME

Not everyone can just relax and let go of the way of life they were accustomed to before the baby was born.

For some new mothers, holding onto habits such as taking the time to shower and dress in the morning or sitting down to dinner with their partners in the evening are emotional anchors that give them the patience to cope with the constant needs of a newborn. A house with some order also gives this Mom the peace of mind she needs to be able to rest according to doctor's orders rather than scrambling around while the baby sleeps trying to clean up the mess made while he or she was awake.

It's wiser to provide a semblance of household and personal order for this mother than to try and talk her out of her needs. One way to help her is to find someone who will provide regular help in the house and give the new mother some time to herself.

Most people will advise the new mother that help at home is an absolute necessity, but what kind of help will be *helpful* is an extremely personal decision, both for financial and emotional reasons. Some women interview and hire infant nurses long before they deliver only to find that they don't want anyone else taking care of the baby; they want to do it themselves. And some women are positive that they want their privacy and time alone with the baby to become acquainted only to find that because of their lack of energy and soreness following delivery they'd prefer to have some professional help for the first few weeks.

Since no woman knows how she's going to feel after delivery or how her baby will feel, it's extremely difficult to make plans for running the household until the delivery. Therefore, while it behooves any imminent mother to find out what her options are for help at home from relatives or professionals, it also is wise to put off the final decision until after the baby is born, if at all possible. Once you're home, you'll have a better feel for whether or not you really want your mother or sister to move in for two weeks. Is she really going to be a help or is she going to drive you crazy? You'll also know whether or not you want help with the baby or help with the house or both. Some new mothers need a housekeeper, some a nurse, some the support of a family member, and some a babysitter just to give them a few hours to bathe at leisure, meet a friend for lunch, or dine alone with their partner.

If you decide to go it alone without any regular hired or family help, make sure that you don't get yourself so dug in at home between housework and mothering that you begin to feel isolated and overwhelmed. Make definite plans to visit friends and relatives during the week or to have them visit you. Sometimes it's easier to let an old friend or relative rather than a stranger babysit for the first time, so don't be shy about asking for an hour or so on your own.

You also should try to make some new acquaintances with other women who have newborns. The gathering place for neighborhood mothers that you probably noticed during your pregnancy is a good place to strike up a new relationship. You also might want to touch base with the childbirth classmates to whom you were closest. If neither of these alternatives is attractive or realistic, you might want to call your obstetrician or midwife to find out if there are any resources for new parents in your community that would put you in contact with other mothers of newborns.

Keep in mind that your initial decision for one kind of help or another isn't irrevocable. If you find that your nurse is intrusive, or your mother—well-meaning as she may be—just not the kind of help you need, speak up. Exchange the nurse for a housekeeper, or your mother for a nurse. If you find that being alone with the baby is too much to handle, don't be shy about arranging for professional or familial help to get you past the early mothering energy crisis.

MEG

I'd always been slim. So I assumed that after having the baby I'd go right back into my old clothes. That wasn't the case, though. First, the nursing itself had a big effect on my figure. My size "A" breasts were a full size "C." The muscles in my abdomen also had no tone. My stomach was flabby and stuck out and I had no waistline at all. I also had some extra weight on my hips. So I didn't fit into my old clothes at all during the whole time I was nursing. Weight loss was very slow, as was regaining muscle tone. I'd say I was in my maternity clothes certainly up to and even past the three-month mark. They fit where my "prebaby" clothes didn't. I thought it would be a waste to buy big clothes just for the postpartum months when I was between figures, so I just kept on wearing my maternity clothes.

STEPHANIE

I didn't gain much weight except in my stomach, so it wasn't long after the baby was born that I was back in my old clothes. Even with nursing, I could wear most of my "prebaby" clothes by the end of the first few weeks of motherhood. It wasn't that I went on a starvation diet or anything. I just snapped back into shape.

7

DIET AND WEIGHT LOSS

Losing weight is one of the most emotional issues new mothers face after their return home. You might be ready for getting up in the middle of the night, for tending to your newborn's every need, and for feeling sore and fatigued, but you may not be ready to face yourself in the mirror without your clothes on. Somehow that immense belly protruding in front of you in late pregnancy minimizes weight gains of twenty-five, thirty, or even forty pounds. As the uterus returns to its normal size during the first six weeks, however, the padded hips, arms, back, and loose belly all begin to emerge from their camouflage.

Although a minority of you will fit back into your prepregnant clothes after the first six weeks, the majority barely will be able to pull your jeans past your knees at a time when the books on childbirth predict you'll be back to normal.

This discrepancy between the predicted weight loss and the actual outcome can be very demoralizing. Women who were proud of their growing bodies now are ashamed of the extra girth and begin recriminating themselves for eating too much during pregnancy. They may punish themselves by not buying any new clothes until they are back into a size six or eight or ten. They may try to restrict their calorie intake too drastically, thereby compromising their nutrition at a time when they need a good diet in order to recuperate at the same time they nurture their newborns.

What you need is a realistic time frame for weight loss that reflects the changes in recommended weight gain during pregnancy that have occurred in the last generation. Here it is:

> It takes nine months to get there and nine months to get back.

Nine months. Not six weeks. Expect it to take nine months to get your figure back. If you get it back sooner, terrific. If it takes you a year or eighteen months, don't worry about it. Nine months is the average, not the rule.

WEIGHT LOSS

By now you have heard the miracle stories of your friend's cousin and other amazing women who went home *thinner* than before pregnancy. You also have been regaled with horror stories about the aunt or friend of a friend who gained sixty pounds during her pregnancy and went home forever forty pounds heavier. Since weight loss is such an emotional issue for most women, these exaggerated stories tend to be given more significance than they probably are due. Even though you *know* that you shouldn't expect to look like your old self for some time, you still may feel insecure about how quickly you're dropping pounds and getting back into your old clothes.

When faced with your spreading bottom, saggy arms, and protruding belly, you can keep despair at bay by reminding yourself of some pertinent facts concerning weight gain, pregnancy, and weight loss.

Your mother probably was told not to gain more than fifteen or eighteen pounds during a pregnancy. Today, we know that the healthiest babies are born to women who gain about twenty-five or thirty pounds, and many mothers tend to gain five or ten pounds more than that. Even if your baby is two pounds heavier at birth than your mother's was, he or she is not going to make up for the extra ten or twenty pounds you gained during pregnancy. Many women lose fifteen to twenty pounds in the hospital and then another five or so at home. Thus, if you gained between thirty and thirty-five pounds, you're going to take home ten to fifteen pounds of extra fat on your hips, your back, and your upper arms. That's where women gain weight and where it's hardest to lose it.

During the first six weeks of recovery, there are at least three factors working against weight loss: One important factor is the age of the new mother. Many new mothers today are older than their counterparts in the last generation. One of the fastest growing populations of first-time mothers is in the thirty- to thirty-five-year-old age group. Losing weight is more difficult for older women because of changes in metabolism associated with aging. Thus, a twenty-five-year-old woman having her first baby is going to have an easier time losing her excess weight than a thirty-five-year-old woman having her first baby.

Another factor having a negative influence on weight loss is the lack of physical activity in the first one or two months. Most mothers are tired and spend a lot of time in bed as their doctors tell them to. Bed rest is necessary for your recovery, but it doesn't help you lose weight. A key factor in any successful weight loss program is regular, rigorous exercise, which helps the dieter expend more calories than she takes in during the day. The new mother, however, won't be ready for a regular strenuous exercise program for several more weeks.

The third factor that can affect the ability to lose weight is the biochemical change going on in the body after childbirth. The change in hormone levels back to a regular cycle can take a few weeks to a few months, depending on the individual woman's body chemistry and whether or not she's breastfeeding. (Breastfeeding usually keeps a woman in a hormonal limbo between pregnancy and her normal cycle.) Most women find it hard to lose weight during the period of hormonal fluctuation following a birth. However, as the body gets back into its normal rhythms, the weight begins to come off easier. It's important to remember that every woman's body returns to its normal hormonal cycle at a different rate, so weight loss in the early months postpartum varies greatly from one woman to the next.

In the first six weeks, then, don't be dismayed if your weight loss is negligible. On the other hand, don't fall into the trap of thinking that nothing is going to help so you might as well let good eating habits be hanged. Many new mothers find that they snack on fast foods high in fat or sugar while they're home alone with their newborns and that they actually gain weight in the first six weeks of motherhood. A weight gain just pushes you further from your goal of recovering your figure. Eventually that goal may seem unattainable as the new mother gets heavier while other women at her stage are beginning to lose weight or at least are holding their own.

To prevent weight gain and start on the way back to your prebaby figure, you'll need to watch your food intake carefully.

DIET

The first six weeks after delivery is not the time to cut down dramatically on your calorie intake. You need a balanced, nutritious daily diet that will help you recover from the birth. However, a balanced diet doesn't need to be fattening. In fact, a good diet rich in fresh fruits and vegetables, lean meats, fish, and whole grains, but low in fats and sugar, will probably encourage weight loss over time. If a new mother finds that she's gaining rather than maintaining or losing weight, her problem probably has more to do with poor eating habits than postpartum hormone fluctuations. Eating habits can deteriorate during the first few weeks of motherhood for a variety of reasons. Here are some common pitfalls and ways to avoid them:

Cooking is a luxury that few new parents can afford. The demands of the baby make it impossible to prepare, eat and clean up after a meal. Many new parents opt for takeout or frozen foods to tide them over the first two or three months of parenthood. Takeout food doesn't have to be fattening, but if the menus for the week are based on fried chicken, french fries, large cokes, and double hamburgers, the calories—and the pounds—are going to mount up. Instead of calorie-laden foods such as these, the new mother might opt for some of the "light" (e.g. Lean Cuisine) frozen dinners now being offered by several manufacturers. These have a combination of nutritious foods in them but are lower in calories than the more standard frozen meat pies or fried chicken. Chinese food that combines vegetables and protein also can be a nutritious takeout dinner that tastes good and is low in fats and starches. If you want to order chicken, try buying a roasted chicken from the supermarket delicatessen rather than fried chicken. In short, when you're depending largely on convenience foods for the first few weeks of parenthood, make sure that the foods you order give you as much food value for the calories as possible. Stay away from "empty" calories in sugary, fatty, or starchy foods.

Snacking can be a big problem for new mothers who spend a lot of time at home during the first few weeks. While she's trying to work out a daily routine with her newborn, the new mother is likely to eat on the run, grabbing a mouthful of something whenever she passes the refrigerator. She really doesn't have the time or energy to prepare a meal and sit down to eat it.

Snacking throughout the day isn't a very satisfying way to eat, and it can lead to weight gain if the snacks are high in calories. Try to stick to three meals a day (unless you're nursing, when six mini-meals may be recommended; see "For the Breastfeeding Mother," p. 138). Meals can be fast and simple if the ingredients going in them are readily available and need little preparation. For breakfast, instant hot cereal that you mix in a bowl topped with fresh fruit and low-fat milk can give you a good start on the day. Fresh fruits with cottage cheese and yogurt sprinkled with wheat germ also takes little time to make. Whole grain breads with canned tunafish or salmon salad and a cut up tomato make a quick lunch. A bowl of soup out of a can with some Parmesan cheese sprinkled on top along with whole wheat toast and a piece of fruit can make a fast, healthy lunch as well.

If you get hungry between meals, snack on fresh fruit and vegetables, a glass of low-fat milk, or if you have a yen for something sweet, an uncoated frozen yogurt bar. Stay away from sodas, potato chips, cookies, cake, and even "health food" snacks such as granola bars made mostly of fats and sugar. These foods give you a lot of calories but very little of the nutrition that your body needs now.

If well-wishers have given you five boxes of chocolate truffles and a few pounds of your favorite chocolate chip cookies, keep one piece of candy and one cookie from each box and send the rest on to your partner's office for a celebration. Keeping a cache of cookies and candy in the house can only spell trouble for the mother who is trying to keep her weight under control.

Pregnant woman usually have increased appetites that go along with their need for about three hundred calories extra a day. New mothers who are not breastfeeding, however, don't need those extra calories. Nonetheless, they may be used to eating larger portions of food than they did before they were pregnant. Some reeducation in what amount of food equals a serving often is necessary. Try using the portion sizes given in the box below as a guideline. Then measure out your meals for one day using a small food scale and measuring cup. This will help retrain your eye to what a normal portion should look like and prevent you from being overgenerous on your own plate.

FOOD	SERVINGS PER DAY
Milk (equivalent to calcium in 1 cup, e.g. 1 cup plain yogurt, 1¼ oz. hard cheese or 2 cups cottage cheese)	2
Meat (equivalent to protein in 2–3 oz. lean meat, poultry, or fish, e.g. 2–3 oz. of hard cheese, 2–3 eggs, or 1–1½ cups cooked dried beans and peas.	2
Vegetables and fruits (½ cup cut up, 1 medium-size piece fruit or vegetable)	4
Bread and cereal (1 slice bread, ½ cup cooked cereal, pasta, or rice, or 1 oz. dry cereal)	4

The box above also gives you the recommended daily allowances for adults of the four basic food groups: milk, meat, vegetables and fruits, breads and cereals. Although you should eat foods from all of the groups during the day, your choices in these categories will have a great influence on your caloric intake for the day. If you make a habit of eating bread slathered with peanut butter and sweetened yogurt for lunch rather than dining on a piece of sparingly buttered whole wheat toast, water-packed tuna, a salad, a cup of skim milk, and a banana, you're going to end up with less satisfaction and more calories— not a good combination for weight loss.

These guidelines are for everyday eating. We all want to splurge once in a while, and there's no reason why a new mother shouldn't enjoy a piece of cake or pie or an ice cream sundae occasionally. In fact, some specialists in weight loss say that an occasional indulgence staves off sweet binges that occur after long periods of abstinence from sweets. Problems don't start until snack foods, candy, and ice cream become the rule rather than the exception.

FOR THE BREASTFEEDING MOTHER

You've probably heard both sides of the nursing and weight loss story. One side suggests that nursing is the best weight reduction plan for the postpartum woman. After all, you expend a thousand calories a day producing milk for your baby, so it only stands to reason that your postpartum weight will dissolve while you nurse.

The other side of the story, however, maintains that weight loss is much harder for the nursing mother. She seems to hold onto her pregnancy weight longer than the bottlefeeding mother and only starts to lose weight after she weans.

As it happens, both sides of this story are true. For some women, weight loss occurs rapidly during breast-feeding. These women drop pounds effortlessly while eating a complete diet for lactating mothers. However, far more nursing mothers experience the opposite effect. While they are nursing, the padding they acquired during pregnancy seems to resist the most conscientious weight loss efforts. Why some nursing women often hold on to the last ten or so pounds they gained during pregnancy hasn't been explained. However, one hypothesis suggests that the lactating mother, much like the pregnant woman, develops an adjusted metabolism that stores as much food as possible (in the form of fatty tissue) to ensure an adequate nutrient supply for milk production. After weaning, the woman's metabolism returns to normal and she finds it possible to lose weight.

Since sluggish weight loss is such a common experience, you shouldn't be concerned if your weight is at a standstill while you're breastfeeding. Just make sure that you're not getting heavier. Be reassured that with good eating habits you'll begin to lose the padding on your arms, back, hips, and thighs as you wean your baby in later months.

Breastfeeding mothers have increased nutritional needs similar to those they had during pregnancy. In order to produce enough milk without depleting their own body's supplies of nutrients, they need to add about five hundred calories a day in calcium, protein, and vitamin-rich foods. The following is a guide to daily dietary recommendations for a nursing mother.

NUTRITIONAL GUIDELINES
FOR NURSING MOTHERS

FOOD GROUP	COMMENTS
Fruits and vegetables (*5 or more ½ cup servings a day*	Include at least: *1 serving of a good source of vitamin A every other day* (e.g. apricots, broccoli, cantaloupe, carrots, beet greens, chard, collards, kale, mustard greens, spinach, turnip greens, pumpkin, sweet potatoes, winter squash)

1 serving of a good source of vitamin C every day (e.g. broccoli, brussels sprouts, cantaloupe, cauliflower, green or sweet red pepper, grapefruit or grapefruit juice, orange or orange juice, tomatoes, chard, collards, kale, mustard greens, spinach, turnip greens, cabbage, strawberries, watermelon)
3 servings of other fruits and vegetables every day

Milk and milk products (4 8 oz. glasses of milk or equivalent in milk products a day)	The following equal 1 8 oz. glass of milk: 1 cup skim milk, low-fat milk, or buttermilk ½ cup evaporated milk (undiluted) 2 1″ cubes or 2 slices cheese ⅓ cup instant powdered milk 1 cup plain yogurt, custard, or milk pudding 3 cups cottage cheese 1-½ cups ice cream
Meat, fish, poultry, eggs, dried beans and peas, nuts (3 2–3 oz. servings)	Some examples of 1 serving are: 2 thin slices beef, pork, lamb, or veal 2 slices luncheon meat 1 hamburger 2 hot dogs 1 whole small fish 1 small fish fillet ⅓ of a 6½ oz. can of tunafish or salmon 2 slices light or dark meat turkey 1 chicken leg ½ chicken breast 1-1½ cup cooked dried beans,

	peas, lentils, or garbanzos (chick peas)
	4–6 tablespoons peanut butter
	2–4 slices cheese
	2 eggs
	2 cups tofu
	6–8 tablespoons nuts or seeds
Whole grain or enriched bread and cereals (4–6 servings)	The following portions equal 1 serving:
	1 slice bread
	1 medium-size muffin
	1 roll or biscuit
	1 tortilla or taco shell
	½–¾ cup cooked or ready-to-eat cereal, such as oatmeal, farina, grits, raisin bran, shredded wheat
	1 cup popcorn (1½ tablespoons unpopped)
	½–¾ cup noodles, spaghetti, rice, bulgur, macaroni
	2 small pancakes
	1 section waffle
	2 graham crackers
	4–6 small crackers
	½ hamburger or hot dog roll
	½ English muffin

Fluid intake is critical to maintaining an adequate milk supply. Nursing mothers should drink two to three quarts of liquid a day (more during very hot weather), one of which should be milk. One way to get all of this fluid into you is to have a tall glass of any nonalcoholic, uncaffeinated beverage at your side to sip every time you sit down to nurse. An occasional beer or cup of coffee is not detrimental, but heavy caffeine or alcohol intake should be avoided.

Some practitioners suggest that you take a multivitamin with iron while you're nursing, while others feel that a balanced diet alone is adequate. Whether you take a supplement or not, you should still be trying to optimize the nutrient content of the food you choose at every meal. Supplements don't take the place of a good diet, they are only meant to *supplement* your nutrient intake.

Six mini-meals rather than three regular meals often are suggested for nursing mothers. Most nursing mothers need the frequent caloric intake, but watch out for two common problems with this mini-meal schedule: eating too much at each meal and eating on the run.

You don't want to get in the habit of eating six big meals a day. Make sure you serve yourself light meals each time rather than six full-size meals or you're likely to go over your recommended caloric intake for a day and start to put on weight. Also, if you're eating six times a day, you may decide to forget the formalities and just grab something from the refrigerator whenever you feel hungry. Such continual grazing, however, may leave you feeling less satisfied than a prepared meal would, and often leads to more snacking. If you're not keeping track, it's easy to snack your way through considerably more food—and more calories—than would be consumed in the six recommended mini meals. Take the time to sit down and eat your meals during the day. Not only will you enjoy your food more, but you'll probably appreciate the break from your mothering duties, also.

SLOW PROGRESS

Since so much pressure is placed on a woman to be a certain physical shape in our culture, reassurance that gradual weight loss is healthy and to be expected after pregnancy seems empty. You know that, too, but you're still aware of the concern your friends and family are starting to show over your weight.

If your weight doesn't drop dramatically during the first six weeks, you're likely to feel that somehow you're responsible for maintaining the increased poundage—especially since more and more of your friends who have babies as old as yours are packing away their maternity clothes in exchange for some of their looser regular clothing. You might want to keep a diary of your eating habits for a few days to make sure that you're not eating more than you think you are. Do you grab something to eat out of the refrigerator every time you get a bottle to warm up? Do you always eat a cracker or cookie with your beverage when you're nursing? When you sit in the park, do you always end up eating something with the rest of the mothers on the bench? These are common eating pitfalls for new mothers, and they can contribute to a slowdown in weight loss or even a weight gain. If your eating diary indicates that you're snacking without thinking between your planned meals, you should make an effort to break the habit and get back to your regular healthy diet.

If, after reviewing your eating habits, you conclude that your weight loss is just proceeding at a slower pace than some other mothers you know, don't try to speed up your progress with drastic methods such as refusing to buy new clothes until you can fit into your old size or going on a fad diet which drastically reduces your caloric and nutritional intake. Such spartan measures won't encourage a weight loss.

Punishing yourself by not buying transitional clothes until you're back into your regular size will only make you feel more unattractive than you are. *You* might think that you look hugely overweight when comparing your figure now to your prepregnant figure. However, to everyone else, you might look perfectly normal if your clothes are flattering. By insisting on wearing your maternity clothes, you might be making yourself look much heavier than you actually are and you won't have the satisfaction of the seeing the effects of your gradual weight loss. Buying a few basic outfits to carry you through the transition from postpartum to normal weight will help you look your best and may help you keep your postpartum weight in proper perspective.

As for diet aids and fad diets that depend on nutritionally unsound eating habits for a quick weight loss, most health professionals agree that these methods are neither safe nor effective as permanent weight loss methods. Postpartum women may find them especially debilitating since they need a healthy diet to give them energy for mothering while continuing to recover from pregnancy and childbirth.

So, what can you do when you're panicking about your weight after your six-week checkup?

Keep reminding yourself that every woman has a unique weight gain and weight loss pattern during and after a pregnancy. Yours may be a little faster or slower than others', but as long as you're gradually losing rather than gaining, you'll eventually return to your normal weight. If you need reassurance of this fact when your weight loss seems slow and uneven, keep a few pictures of yourself in the last month of pregnancy on hand to show how far you've come.

Exercise regularly. Exercise will strengthen and firm your muscles and promote weight loss, both of which will hasten the return of your prepregnant figure. While you can't start back to a regular workout during the early weeks postpartum, don't discount your long walks with the baby carriage. They not only provide a good source of gentle exercise, but they get you out of the house and away from the refrigerator as well.

Eat well, but carefully. Some new mothers are so disillusioned after eating carefully for a few months with little weight loss that they overindulge in sweets and fats. The weight gain from such overindulgence will only add to the problem. When you're feeling frustrated by how long your body is taking to get back into shape, call a sympathetic friend before you run out for ice cream. Words of encouragement often can assuage frustration as well as a sweet snack, and they don't carry the price of a setback from your goal.

Buy one or two transitional outfits that flatter your figure now. Don't automatically buy your usual style of clothing a few sizes larger than normal. You might find that such a choice merely emphasizes the fact that you're a couple of sizes larger than usual. Instead, try on different styles to see what makes you look your best now. Two or three outfits made up of neutral separates and dressed up with the accessories you already own can go a long way in making you feel better about yourself and not as desperate to be back in your prepregnancy clothes.

Weight is such an obsession in this culture that many

of you probably spent a great part of your pregnancy planning how you would take off the pounds you were putting on from one month to the next. In fact, you don't need to worry so much. In the majority of cases, pregnancy weight is temporary. If you're eating in a reasonable fashion that doesn't lead to postpartum weight gain, you can count on your weight to decrease slowly until you're within a few pounds of your original weight without a lot of worrisome dieting. Some women have trouble with the last five or seven pounds, but the other twenty-five or so usually aren't a problem.

After the first six weeks have passed, both baby and mother are more settled into their routines. The lives of new mothers vary greatly after this point. Some are already going back to work. Some are making the decision not to return to their jobs. Despite different life circumstances, however, each new mother will begin an earnest attempt to regain control of her life at this point, which is the underlying theme of the next few months of motherhood.

PART 3

SIX WEEKS TO THREE MONTHS

DRAKE

I made a concerted effort to avoid business travel in the first few months after Tucker was born. I also tried to get home from work as soon as possible, put in as little overtime as possible. Because I lived an hour and a half from work, the earliest I would get home would be around 7:30 or 8:00. What Heather worked out was a schedule whereby Tucker would nurse at about 6:00 and then have a nap until I came home. Then we'd have an hour or so before he went to bed for the night. It worked out well.

I see work differently now. In a sense, I like knowing I am doing a different part of what needs to be done for Tucker than Heather is. I'm bringing home the bread. My priorities have been realigned. I feel a tremendous amount of responsibility now. I went out and bought insurance, you know, to make sure that Tucker and Heather would be taken care of if something happened to me. It never occurred to me to buy life insurance before this.

JUDY

At six weeks, I remember that we went out alone for the first time. That might not sound like a big deal to most people, but Devon had colic and we just hadn't dared leave him with anyone because of his incessant, blood-curdling screaming. Finally, we did entrust him to an experienced babysitter. We were supposed to go out to dinner and then a movie, but we didn't get to the movie. We were just too nervous about leaving Devon with a sitter that long. _We_ could handle his crying, but we didn't know if a stranger could.

Devon's colic ruled our lives for the first three months of his life. We made great headway after the six-week mark because we could get him to sit in the swing or the rocking infant seat long enough for us to eat dinner together. Before that time, one of us was carrying him constantly. And then, little by little over the next six weeks, the crying jags became shorter and less intense.

Jim and I didn't really have much of a relationship during those early months. We didn't fight more or less. We just didn't relate to one another. Each of us was just struggling to get through the endless days of continual screaming in our own way. However, when the colic subsided, we were okay. We didn't love Devon any less for having had those two and a half terrible months. We were just glad to be able to get on with our life as a family.

SHAUNA

It didn't dawn on me until weeks after Alex was born that I would have him every day of my life. Somehow I didn't comprehend the notion of someone being a part of my life every minute of every day whether I'm physically with him or not. When I'm with Alex, my attention is focused on him, and when I'm away from him at work, I'm thinking about him. This part of mothering never dawned on me. I never thought I would have a baby all the time. I thought I would be a mother when I was at home and a professional when I was at work, just like I'm a wife when I'm at home, but really turn my attention away from that role when I'm at work. Motherhood isn't like that. It's all the time.

8

GETTING BACK ON SCHEDULE

After the six-week checkup, many new mothers become impatient with the unfocused rhythm of their lives. The seamless days and nights of nurturing that are unpunctuated by normal benchmarks—reading the morning paper *in the morning*, showering and dressing before breakfast, and going to and from work with the other office migrants—lose their blush of newness. Some women begin to feel that they're drifting away from the real world in their cocoon of new motherhood. The drain of being on call all day to manage every detail of their infants' lives begins to wear on them. They want the luxury of setting and achieving even small personal goals again, such as exercising at the health club twice a week, getting *anyplace* on time, or reviving friendships that have been neglected. They want to get back to normal.

This budding sense of urgency to get control of life again is increased by pressure from society for the new mother to integrate her mothering duties into her previous lifestyle. People are not as lenient about lateness and other social indiscretions as they were during the first weeks after the baby was born. The new mother is supposed to have adjusted her lifestyle so as to make her childcare routine fit effortlessly into her old routine. The assumption is that mothering an infant is so basic and simple that it shouldn't be taking up much of time after a routine gets established. That's a favorite phrase, "Once you get into a routine, you'll be okay."

In fact, most new mothers by this time have found that mothering is anything but simple and basic. A newborn comes into the world with a complex personality that the mother has to decipher without the aid of verbal communication. A feeding, changing, or bath is not just a mechanical gesture but a time of gratifying interaction between mother and child when each becomes slightly more familiar with the other's gestures of affection, sense of humor, or expressions of frustration. Most new mothers don't want to sandwich their mothering in between everything else. Instead, they want to push back other obligations in order to enjoy mothering rather than hurry through it.

The notion of finding a routine also is somewhat fallacious. No doubt you'll be trying in the long run to guide your baby into sleeping at night, being awake during the day, napping at regular hours, and eating at regular intervals. However, the patterns that emerge in your baby's life in the first months are extremely transient. You probably will find that any routine you set up is disrupted within days of its inception. In fact, a great part of the postpartum physical and emotional wear comes from the constant adjustment to the baby's changing schedules.

Most of you probably will find the early attempts at combining motherhood with any of your other roles draining. You never seem to have any time off. You never seen to be able to finish what you start or to do one thing as well as you want. Most of you will discover—after making yourself crazy trying to do everything you did before you had a baby—that getting *back* to normal is impossible. Instead, what you will be doing in the next few months is creating a new "normal" for yourself that includes your role as mother.

As you integrate motherhood into your postpartum lifestyle, make sure that your personal needs are being addressed in your new schedule. Too many new mothers relinquish the few hours of private time they used to have to collect their thoughts in favor of accomplishing more during the day. That private time, however, is critical to a new mother's well-being. After a few weeks of scheduling your days from the moment you wake up until you go to bed at night, you will most likely feel physically and emotionally overwhelmed. Leave an hour somewhere during the day when you can take a walk, go to a health club, take a dance class, read in the tub, or visit a friend. If you're a morning person, the hour can be before you and/or your partner go to work. If you're an evening person, ask your partner to take over baby duty at the end of the day and get yourself out of the house for a while. Remember that the time you take will benefit your family as well as yourself. Even a short break from the daily routine—if it's regular—can refuel your emotional reserves and keep you from feeling that you're being overwhelmed by other people's needs.

Though your experience of the first three months of motherhood will be shaped by your individual circumstances, some general physical concerns will be shared by many of you.

BODY SHAPE

Whether you're three or thirteen pounds overweight during the first six months, you may be dismayed at your postpartum figure. Even if the scale tips close to your regular weight, you may find that you just don't fit into the clothes you wore before your pregnancy. Shirts gap between the buttons, skirts don't button, and pants are too tight to be comfortable. You have to remember that weight is not the only factor in your body returning to its former shape. Muscle tone has a lot to do with your figure, as does redistribution of weight and skin elasticity.

MUSCLE TONE   Good muscle tone refers to muscles that are resilient; after they are stretched, they return to a resting position that provides a strong bulwark to the structures they support. Poor muscle tone suggests muscles that are weak and slack and provide little support. The physical shape most of us aspire to is dictated by good muscle tone that manifests itself in a flat belly, narrow waist, and sleek hips. Muscle tone does not improve much on its own. You have to exercise to build up strength and resilience. (See Chapter 10).

SKIN ELASTICITY   Your skin's remarkable elasticity is what enables your body to accommodate your growing uterus and swelling breasts, and then return to its original shape after birth. This is particularly true of new mothers in their twenties. New mothers in their thirties and forties may find that the elasticity of their skin is decreasing somewhat. Their skin may take longer to firm up after birth, and it may remain less firm than it was before. Unlike your muscles, your skin's tone cannot be influenced by exercising. Skin has a natural elasticity which cannot be improved through exercise.

Although the skin has great stretching capabilities, there is a limit to its elasticity. When the skin is stretched beyond its limit during pregnancy, a permanent stretch mark will appear. Initially it will be red, but over time it will shrink and become a silvery white mark. Most women notice stretch marks on their abdomen and breasts.

REDISTRIBUTION OF WEIGHT

During your pregnancy, you probably accumulated fatty tissue in your thighs, buttocks, hips, and perhaps upper back. The hormone progesterone, produced in large amounts throughout your pregnancy, is partly responsible for this accumulation, as it encourages fat storage. After you deliver, the circulating progesterone level falls off and your tendency to accumulate fat drops back to normal.

Encouraging the accumulation of fat is the body's way of ensuring that you will have enough stored nutrients to care for and feed your baby after birth, even if food and assistance is scarce. Most of you, however, will have plenty of help and good food to eat, obviating the need for this excess padding. Since it is not burned up for emergency energy, the fat that is already stored will take several months to be reabsorbed by the body or used in the course of daily activity.

New mothers tend to be most self-conscious about their breasts, abdomen, and hips.

BREASTS   The glandular milk-producing tissue that developed in your breasts during pregnancy has made them significantly fuller. Each of them has gained about a pound and a half by the time milk production begins. Even if you are not breastfeeding, your breasts are going to take time to return to their prepregnant condition because the extensive milk duct system has to be reabsorbed by the body.

Most of you will notice significant changes in your breasts. They probably will fit into the same cup size, but they are likely to be less firm and uplifted. The breast shape often is somewhat flatter at the chest wall and fuller near the nipple. The skin that stretched to accommodate the extra breast tissue now may look a little like an empty pocket. Don't be too dismayed by the flabby look of your breasts. In the next few months your breasts will firm up slowly as the stretched skin regains its tone.

If you are breastfeeding, you're probably unable even to button any of your old shirts and blouses. The initial engorgement may be behind you, but your breasts still are fuller than normal. As you reach your third month of nursing, however, you may notice the fullness diminishing. As was mentioned in Chapter 5, this lack of fullness doesn't represent a loss of milk. In fact, it is a sign that your milk production is well established and functioning efficiently. Your breasts may continue to decrease in size from now until you wean even though your milk production may be increasing to meet the needs of your growing baby. Some of you may return to your normal bra size while breastfeeding. However, most women find that their breasts remain slightly fuller than normal until they've finished nursing completely.

ABDOMEN   You probably were blaming involution for your pot belly all through the first six weeks, but what can you blame now? Your uterus is tucked back under your pelvic bone, yet your belly still seems bloated. You may find that you still don't fit into any regular clothing, regardless of size, because you still have no waist at all.

Much of the bloated condition of your belly and waist is due not to added weight (though that will play a role) but to overstretched muscle and skin tissue that isn't firm enough to return to its previous shape. Remember that your abdomen skin and muscles had to stretch enormously to accommodate your pregnancy. Abdominal muscles in particular lose a great deal of their resiliency during pregnancy because they are stretched far beyond the point where they can snap back into their normal supportive position. After birth, they will not remain as stretched as they were around your enlarged uterus, but they will return only to a slack resting position, as evidenced by the soft protruding belly that most of you notice.

The gentle postpartum exercises suggested for the first six weeks of motherhood can begin the firming and strengthening of the abdominal muscles, but after the first six weeks more strenuous exercises may in in order to regain your abdominal muscle tone (see Chapter 10).

How long your skin and muscle take to return to normal will depend on how much the tissues had to stretch, how much you exercise, your condition before you were pregnant, and your age. At the end of this three months, some of you will fit into your regular clothes. Others, whose skin and muscle tone as well as weight take longer to return to normal, can gain some satisfaction from seeing less of a bulging tummy and even a little dip around the waist where none existed just a couple of months ago.

HIPS Most women notice that their hips become substantially padded during pregnancy. For some reason, this added bulk often is the most difficult to lose. Even when waist-cinching skirts and regular blouses fit, a favorite pair of pants still resists being pulled over the broadened hips.

What can you do? Walking and biking can hasten the return of slender hips. Even with extra exercise, however, many women lose this bulk around the hips last, so try not to be too concerned about how slow your progress is—as long as there is progress. Every few weeks try on your favorite pants. Are they getting a little closer to fitting? If so, you're doing all right.

RETURN OF THE MENSTRUAL CYCLE

Your menstrual cycle is dependent on a series of hormonal triggers that encourage ovulation, prepare the uterus for implantation of the egg, and if fertilization doesn't occur, allow the unfertilized egg and excess uterine lining to be expelled. During pregnancy, this cycle is suspended. Instead, hormones are released in order to maintain the pregnancy and prepare the body for birth and lactation. The placenta plays a primary role in maintaining the pregnancy by supplying large amounts of estrogen and progesterone. The levels of these two hormones drop suddenly after the placenta is delivered, and they are inhibited from further production by the immediate release of prolactin—the hormone responsible for initiating and maintaining milk production. Prolactin is produced throughout life but only allowed to be released after birth to promote milk production and prevent ovulation. Until milk production is discouraged, prolactin will maintain this hormonal mock-menopause. However, as soon as milk production ceases, prolactin release once again is suppressed, and the normal cyclical production of estrogen and progesterone begins again, resulting in the resumption of the menstrual cycle.

If you bottlefeed, you can expect your period to return in about six to eight weeks. The onset of menstruation for nursing mothers is much more difficult to predict. Most often, the first postpartum period won't occur until after weaning. However, some of you may get your first period in the later months of breastfeeding, when your feedings are less frequent.

The first few cycles postpartum usually are unpredictable. You may find that your first period arrives suddenly with none of the usual premenstrual and menstrual symptoms you were used to before pregnancy. Your period may be shorter than normal, but may recur after only two or three weeks. The menstrual flow may be either lighter or heavier than you were used to before birth. These anomalies in your cycle usually are no cause for concern and will cease once your body's mechanism for regulating the monthly hormonal cycle of ovulation reestablishes itself.

> However, if you find that the bleeding in the first two or three days of your postpartum cycle is *much* heavier than you were accustomed to before you had your baby, consult your physician.

If you suffered from dysmenorrhea (painful cramps) before you became pregnant, you probably will notice that the disabling cramps are much less severe if not entirely absent following childbirth. Other symptoms that accompany menstruation, such as bloating, moodiness, and headache, are likely to return when your hormonal cycle is restored to normal.

CONTRACEPTIVES

Don't be misled into thinking that the absence of a period makes pregnancy impossible. Remember that ovulation takes place two weeks *before* your period, so you could get pregnant two weeks before your first period following birth.

If you are bottlefeeding, you have the option of using oral contraceptives or one of the variety of barrier methods (diaphragms, sponges or condoms with spermicidal gels, foams, or creams). If you are breastfeeding, you'll be advised against oral contraceptives until you wean your baby.

If you used a diaphragm before you became pregnant, don't assume that you can go back to using the same one. Some women need to be refitted with a new size following birth as the cervix's shape changes. Make sure you have your size checked by your midwife or obstetrician before resuming sexual relations.

If this is the first time you are trying barrier contraceptives, make sure that you sample a variety of brands and types. You may prefer creams to foams, or the fragrance of one gel over another. You may prefer sponges to diaphragms or condoms to them all. You also may find that you prefer to vary your barrier method according to your circumstances.

When you resume sexual relations, don't assume that the contraceptive solution you used before will be right for you now. Those of you who have healing episiotomies might find that inserting a diaphragm is painful during the early months postpartum. Condoms—well lubricated— might be not only more comfortable but also more convenient for spur-of-the-moment romance. If you were accustomed to using gels, you might find now that creams afford you the lubrication you're lacking in the first few months after birth due to hormonal changes (see Chapter 9). In other words, what you liked before you became pregnant might not work for you as well after birth. You might have to try new products or a combination of products you know to come up with a satisfactory solution to your contraceptive needs.

HAIR LOSS

Hair growth usually occurs in a two-phase cycle. The growth or anagen phase lasts between three and seven years for each hair. During this time, the hair follicle actively produces keratin, the fibrous protein that makes up hair. At the end of the anagen phase, the follicle enters the resting or telogen phase, when growth stops and the hair attached to the follicle eventually falls out. This phase lasts about three to six months, after which time the follicle becomes active again. Normally, about 90 percent of your hair is in the anagen phase and about 10 percent in the telogen phase. However, due to the hormonal changes that occur during pregnancy, almost all of your hair enters the anagen phase, resulting in a thicker, fuller head of hair.

After delivery, as your hormones return to their prepregnant levels, your hair will once again resume its regular cycle of being 90 percent anagenic and 10 percent telogenic. The extra hair that grew during pregnancy will begin to fall out, usually at the end of the third month postpartum. At first, the hairbrush or comb may seem to catch a few more hairs than normal, but after a couple of weeks it may seem as if you're losing fistfuls of hair every time you shampoo. In fact, you are losing quite a bit of hair—all of the extra growth that was stimulated by your pregnancy. Once your hair has returned to its normal thickness—usually within a couple of months—the hair loss will drop off.

A major issue that arises in these months following the six-week checkup is sexual relations. Sex often is profoundly different for a new mother on every level. She frequently is as confused about her ambivalence or change in sexual response as is her partner. In the next chapter, some of the reasons for a new mother's struggle with sex and sexuality will be discussed.

MELINDA

In the first months of motherhood, intimacy was redefined for me in many ways. It took forms other than sex, such as nursing my baby in bed at midnight. That was one of the problems with getting my sex life back on track. But other factors played a role also. I just felt physically mauled all the time—my breasts in particular because I was nursing every couple of hours and breastfeeding was painful for quite a long time. So when I wasn't in some way physically involved with Matthew, I felt as if I just wanted to wrap a blanket around myself and be left alone. I wasn't very receptive physically.

Another problem with intercourse that made me want to avoid sex was how painful it was. I was so dry and tight. Just putting in the diaphragm was painful, so I'd get off to a bad start. Then sex itself just wasn't pleasurable. I'd find that in order to get past the initial discomfort and begin to enjoy myself I'd have to concentrate on relaxing and feeling good. But my mind always wandered, and then Matthew would start to whimper or cry and whatever interest I had in sex would evaporate. I'd want to jump out of bed to see what was wrong. The pull was so strong. But for my husband, the involvement with sex was stronger. He'd say, "Let him cry for a minute until we're finished." We just felt so differently about sex. I just couldn't get wrapped up in it like I did before.

ANDREA

Sex for me is better than it ever was before I had Sarah. My husband and I were so much in our own worlds, we really weren't very close. We lived parallel lives. Our interest in and love for Sarah has really brought us together, and because of our emotional closeness our sexual life is much more satisfying. That's not to say that sex felt great after birth. Even though I had a Cesarean section, penetration still hurt like hell while I was nursing because I was so dry. However, my doctor told me that this was normal and that after I stopped nursing sex would feel good again, so I wasn't too worried. When I stopped nursing, sex *did* feel great again, and I was more interested than ever.

SUSAN

Several months after birth, I still found sex to be intolerably painful. I had had an episiotomy and was concerned that maybe it hadn't healed right. Finally, I went back to my obstetrician and found out that incision hadn't healed perfectly. He gave me estrogen cream to encourage healing and elasticity in the area. If the cream isn't effective, the doctor said that he could perform and repair another episiotomy as a last resort and hope that the new incision would heal better. I'm not looking forward to that, so I'm giving the cream a long trial. I've been using it now for six weeks and sex doesn't seem to hurt as much, but it's still not painless or pleasurable.

9

SEX AFTER BIRTH

The six-week checkup ends the traditional period of abstinence from intercourse following birth. Today, however, many medical practitioners feel that sexual relations may be resumed as early as three to four weeks after birth, depending on whether or not the new mother has passed two important milestones of recovery: (1) healing of the episiotomy and/or lacerations that occurred during childbirth; and (2) cessation of lochia.

The mending of vaginal and perineal tissues following birth may be compromised if intercourse occurs too early. Your practitioner can tell you when you've healed enough to resume sexual relations. However, you don't have to wait the usual six weeks for this information. If you're feeling comfortable and want to have intercourse earlier, ask for an earlier postpartum checkup.

The end of the lochia signals that your uterus and cervix probably have recovered from the birth. At this point, the cervix should be completely closed, which is necessary to prevent the introduction of bacteria into the uterus during intercourse.

Some new mothers are anxious to return to sexual activity. Their newborn has brought them closer than ever to their partners, and sex is a more profoundly satisfying expression of love than it ever had been. Some mothers also find that their experience with pregnancy and childbirth has made them more comfortable with their bodies than they were in the past. They now can give themselves over to sexual arousal in a way that was impossible before. In addition, many woman notice that orgasm is easier to attain, an experience that is related to the increased circulation of blood to the genitals that occurs during pregnancy and continues after as well. The increase in circulation is a result of the development of a more complex circulatory system in the pelvic area during pregnancy. This increase in circulation allows for faster arousal and more intense orgasms in some women.

Many other mothers, however, are still too sore or tired to look forward to sexual intercourse. Conflicting emotions about the roles of wife and mother also put a kink in the renewal of sexual intimacy. Although they frequently aren't spoken of, these feelings of ambivalence toward sex as well as physical discomfort and lack of arousal all are common experiences for new mothers. Because these problems with sex don't receive the attention that other postpartum experiences do, many new mothers feel as if there is something wrong with them as individuals, and the anxiety fostered by those feelings makes sex an even more tension-filled issue.

Understanding the variety of experiences affecting your sex life after birth may help you return to an active, enjoyable sex life without suffering unnecessarily from doubts about your ability and desire to perform.

DRYNESS

Pain during sex is an almost universal complaint in the first few months after birth, and much of the problem is due to dryness. Normally, when you become aroused, your vagina lubricates itself, making the tissue pliable and making penetration easy and enjoyable. The hormone estrogen is responsible for this lubrication. However, as was mentioned in Chapter 8, estrogen is at a very low level in the new mother's body anywhere from a few weeks to a few months. As a result, she won't lubricate as quickly or as much as she normally would during sexual intercourse. Without this lubrication, the vaginal tissue won't stretch easily and penetration becomes difficult and painful.

Vaginal dryness resolves itself as the estrogen level returns to normal after birth. In mothers who choose to bottlefeed, the problem may last only a couple of months. However, in mothers who nurse vaginal dryness may last as long as breastfeeding continues. As long as the new mother is lactating, her estrogen level will be low.

However long the dryness lasts, a new mother can make sexual intercourse more comfortable by trying the following:

- Give yourself extra time to become aroused. Your natural lubrication needs a little more coaxing during this transitional hormone state.
- Massage the opening to the vagina with vitamin E oil to stretch and lubricate the tissue *before* penetration.
- Ask your practitioner to prescribe estrogen cream which encourages thickening and elasticity of the vaginal walls.
- Use a lubricant such as K-Y jelly on the head of your partner's penis to facilitate penetration.
- Ask your partner to enter slowly so that your vagina has a chance to stretch rather than be forced open.

EPISIOTOMY DISCOMFORT

For many women, the discomfort caused by lack of lubrication is compounded by the still healing episiotomy incision. When you return to your doctor at six weeks and he or she tells you that the incision is healed, that means that the earliest stages of healing—the joining of the tissue—is complete. The nerve endings in the tissue might still be mending, and the scar tissue left by the incision will still be fresh and unyielding, unlike the rest of the vaginal tissue, which, with lubrication, is very elastic. During sexual intercourse, penetration can cause a pulling on the tender scar tissue as well as irritation of the cut nerves in the area, and this combination can be extremely painful.

If you suffer a lot of discomfort the first time you attempt sexual intercourse, you may be afraid that your episiotomy repair was performed incorrectly and that you'll have to endure painful intercourse for the rest of your life.

This is not the case. Keep in mind that the average time for an episiotomy to heal to the point where sex feels normal again is about six *months*, not six weeks. If the discomfort you suffer during intercourse is very severe after your six-week checkup, wait a few more weeks before attempting sex again. During that time, follow these steps to promote healing of the scar tissue:

- After soaking in a warm bath, take some vitamin E oil and massage it into the site of the episiotomy. As you massage, slowly stretch the skin. If you do this massage regularly, you'll help restore the resilience to the scar tissue that is necessary to allow for comfortable penetration.
- Use prescribed estrogen cream to facilitate healing.
- Do your Kegel exercises religiously. Kegels increase the circulation to the episiotomy tissue and promote healing and restoration of muscle tone.
- When you're ready to attempt sex again, soak in your warm bath, massage in the vitamin E oil, and then use your topical anesthetic just at the site of the scar to numb the area temporarily. Then follow the steps recommended above for increasing lubrication.

In extreme circumstances, when sexual intercourse remains too painful to be enjoyable more than a year after birth, reconstructive surgery may be suggested as an alternative. In this procedure, the scar tissue that formed when the initial episiotomy or tear was repaired is surgically removed and the tissue is rejoined. In the majority of cases, the new incision mends adequately, but a few women find that the scar tissue develops again after the second repair. Surgery to remove scar tissue should not be considered lightly as the healing process is often uncomfortable and extended.

CHANGES IN THE VAGINA

Two types of changes in the vaginal canal can be expected, one permanent and one temporary. The temporary change is in the muscle tone. During birth, the vaginal muscles certainly are stretched greatly, and they may continue to feel loose for several months after delivery. However, like the abdominal muscles, the vaginal muscles can be firmed and strengthened through exercise. If you do your Kegel exercises regularly, your vaginal muscle tone can be restored in six months or less.

The permanent changes may occur when the vagina stretched during delivery. The mouth of the vagina may return to a size and shape different from that before birth. Further changes can result from vaginal tears or an episiotomy that requires repair. Scar tissue at the site of the repair or repairs may be rigid and unyielding for many months. Even after the scar tissue has become more elastic, the vagina may not return exactly to its previous condition following childbirth. Most women find that they become accustomed to their postpartum vaginas and feel as satisfied with intercourse as they were before giving birth.

For the few women who find sex unsatisfying after birth because of birth-related vaginal changes, reconstructive surgery to correct vaginal physiology is available but should be considered only as a last resort.

CESAREAN INCISIONS

Like an episiotomy incision, a Cesarean incision may be healed on the surface at six weeks. However, at that time the new mother is still likely to feel soreness and some pain when using the abdominal muscles. Complete healing, when the incision feels normal again, often takes up to a year. Most women who have Cesarean sections are reassured that at least they won't have the soreness of an episiotomy to contend with. However, the dryness that affects all new mothers will also affect the mother who had a Cesarean section. Thus, during sex, the mother delivered by Cesarean section has a twofold problem to deal with—vaginal dryness and abdominal incision soreness.

To start, make sure you follow the advice for vaginal dryness before you attempt intercourse. Then, consider what position is most comfortable for you to recline in and consider adapting that position for sex. Here are some ideas:

- Partner on top: If you're most comfortable flat on your back, your partner can enter you from above. However, to prevent him from putting weight on your incision, ask him to try making love from a kneeling position above you.
- Partner behind: If you are comfortable on one side, your partner can enter you from the back without putting pressure on the incision.
- Partner underneath: If sitting up is comfortable for you, or if it allows you more control over sexual intercourse to prevent discomfort, try a position where you straddle your partner.

FATIGUE

For many women, position, stitches, and dryness are less problematic than exhaustion. Even after the six-week checkup, some new mothers are still sleeping whenever they have the opportunity to make up for the sleep they lose during night feedings and to help them recover. For the many women who return to work six to eight weeks after delivery, the fatigue problem is compounded. They have to keep their regular work schedule as well as tend to the baby at night. Fathers who share the middle-of-the-night feeding duty usually can appreciate the exhaustion felt by the mother, but when sex is put off week after week they nonetheless can become frustrated and angry at being third in line to the baby and the job. And although fathers rarely believe it, mothers also miss the intimate moments they shared before the baby. What can the new parents do?

Too often, the answer to this problem takes the shape of a tired mother finally submitting to sex so that she won't have to hear complaints anymore. However, this kind of sex can hardly be called intimacy and only leads to anger on the mother's part and a greater rift between the new parents.

Rather than making sex a last resort to stop an argument, parents can try to restore physical intimacy as an expression of their affection for one another. Make a date during one of the baby's naps on both days of the weekend when you will take time just to be together and strengthen your bond as a couple. That sounds obvious, but most new parents hustle around catching up on whatever they've neglected when the baby sleeps rather than taking the time to relax together. Sex needn't always be a part of these quiet moments. Having an hour or two to watch a favorite TV show or video movie while tucked in together on the couch can be immensely satisfying. Some couples like to establish a certain ritual they can share, like morning coffee in bed with the baby, or an evening glass of sherry or wine after the baby's in bed—whenever that occurs, or an evening walk just after work, before the obstacles of dinner and baby care take up the whole evening. As parents being to renew their intimacy through these rituals of closeness, sex is more likely to follow as a natural expression of love just as it did before the birth.

LOSS OF LIBIDO

Most new mothers don't expect to feel like femme fatales the night after they come home from the hospital. However, after two or three months have gone by and they don't feel the familiar tingle, flush, and headiness of arousal when they're embraced by their partners, they begin to worry. Does sexual arousal end for a woman after birth? Is it all just mechanical from then on?

For most women, the answer to that question is no. The loss of libido is temporary and will return in time. How much time is individual. Some women need only a couple of months to feel the return of desire, but others only feel faint stirrings many months after the birth.

Loss of libido in new mothers hasn't been studied, so the reasons for this postpartum lull haven't been documented. However, the following are some of the factors mothers feel play a part in their lack of desire:

DIMINISHED AROUSAL Many of you may wonder at the lack of arousal you experience during moments when you surely would have felt excited before birth. The baby is asleep, you're tired though not exhausted, the opportunity for an intimate encounter is at hand, but you can't summon up the physical response you want. If this has happened to you, don't worry. You're not alone.

Masters and Johnson, pioneers in sexual research, conducted a study on the new mother's physiological response showing that arousal may be diminished in the early postpartum period. The study measured the response to sexual stimulation by monitoring the vasocongestion which occurred in the pelvic area. Vasocongestion is caused by an increase in the blood supply to the pelvic area which becomes trapped and results in the swelling of the genital organs. It is an important part of arousal and orgasm for both men and women. The congestion causes and maintains a male's erection when he is aroused and also causes the swelling of the female's clitoris as well as lubrication of the vagina during enjoyable sexual activity. The congestion increases up to the point where orgasm is reached, after which point the blood is released back into the body's circulatory system. If the vasocongestion of the genitals is inadequate, you won't feel a sense of arousal and sexual tension. In Masters and Johnson's study, the mothers, who were four and eight weeks postpartum, didn't experience the vasocongestion or the lubrication normally associated with sexual arousal.

The reason for this diminished response is clear, but psychological as well as physical factors are certain to play a part. Certainly the lower level of estrogen, which leaves the vagina dry and makes intercourse uncomfortable, contributes, as does the unfamiliar feel of the genital area following birth. But the emotional pull of the newborn also takes its toll, as well as the need for private time to sort through your feelings about becoming a mother.

Keep in mind that this inability to become fully aroused just after birth occurs in some, though not all, new mothers. You might take as much pleasure in sex a couple of months after birth as you did before you deliver. Don't assume that you won't enjoy sex. Try it and find out.

Also, remember that this lack of libido is temporary. Once your hormonal cycles are reestablished, your body feels familiar and comfortable again, and motherhood is second nature, your ability to become aroused and have orgasms will return. The time it takes for all of these milestones to be reached, however, varies greatly.

TRANSITION FROM BIRTHING MOTHER TO SEXUAL PARTNER   Towards the end of your pregnancy and while you're delivering, your genitals become the focus of a lot of asexual attention. You're prodded and poked by your doctor and then by hospital staff who are looking for signs of progress during your labor. You might be shaved or have monitors inserted in your vagina. No longer are your genitals a shrouded center of sexual pleasure. Now they are exposed and prepared for the very functional purpose of birthing your baby. Often it takes some time after birth for a new mother to feel like a sexual partner again rather than like a birthing apparatus.

THE NEED TO HAVE HER BODY TO HERSELF   Sharing your body with a developing human being and then giving birth to that person can be an overwhelmingly invasive experience. Many women just want to have their bodies to themselves for a while after what feels like a violation of their privacy. Loss of libido reflects this need to be left alone for a time. However, the sensitivity to physical contact will resolve itself as time distances the new mother from her pregnancy and birth experience, and the desire for sexual contact gradually will return.

CONTACT OVERLOAD   A new mother spends much of her day holding, nuzzling, feeding, and kissing her baby. Most of that time she's happy to be so close to her newborn. However, if there hasn't been a minute in the day when the new mother has had a chance to be by herself, she may feel the need to be physically alone once the baby is down for the night. Unfortunately, that's usually the time when her partner snuggles up for his closeness after being second to the baby all evening. The new mother often shrugs off the hug, which can alienate and even anger her partner. She might begrudgingly give in to an arm over her shoulders just to avoid an argument, but neither partner is getting what they want under those circumstances.

A better way for you to handle contact overload would be to have the father shoulder most of the comforting and holding during the evening so that you get that time off. Use the time to really escape from the family. Take a walk. Have a quick drink with a friend. Lock the bathroom door and take a long bath. Go to the gym and take a swim or an exercise class. After some private time, you're likely to feel more like snuggling up to your partner.

MOTHER VS. WIFE

Some women find their roles as sexual partners difficult to integrate with their roles as asexual mothers. Going from a middle-of-the-night feeding to a middle-of-the-night tryst with a partner can be a difficult transition. This new mother might like to get back to her sexually active life but finds that being bounced back and forth from motherhood duties to partner duties prevents her from feeling comfortable with sex. What might help this new mother is to make a clean break from nurturing, such as going out to dinner or to the movies, which will give her a chance to focus on her relationship with her partner without being distracted by the baby. Sometimes just a dinner by candlelight at home once the baby's down or watching a television movie snuggled up on the couch can help this mother regain her footing as a sexual partner. The important ingredient seems to be attention from the partner *before* the initiation of sex so that the new mother can feel emotionally as well as physically intimate with her partner.

BODY IMAGE

How a woman views herself physically can have a great effect on her sexuality. If a postpartum woman is accustomed to being sleek and firm, the flaccid belly muscles, padded hips and thighs, and pendulous breasts that often are the badges of early motherhood may embarrass her. A woman who had a Cesarean section may feel sensitive about her scar.

If you're feeling flabby and unattractive because your body isn't as it was before you had your baby, remember how far you have come. Consider that just a couple of months ago your belly not only was large enough to throw a shadow over your feet, but it often moved as well. Of course, a few words of encouragement from your partner will go a long way toward making you feel sexually attractive again. However, your partner may be unaware that you're embarrassed or ashamed of your body. He may need you to express your worries about being unattractive sexually before he'll offer the kind of reassurance you need. You might try saying something like, "You know, sometimes I feel like my old sexy self, but then I catch a glimpse of my body in the bedroom mirror and I think you must be having trouble being attracted to me when I look and feel this way."

BREASTFEEDING

Some breastfeeding mothers and their partners find that their feelings about breasts as an erogenous zone change during breastfeeding. Nursing mothers often feel strange sharing their breasts with their newborns and their partners. Fathers often feel the same ambivalence about fondling or suckling the breasts their babies nurse on. Some are curious about breast milk and find it an enjoyable addition to sexual interaction. Others are put off by it. Nursing mothers and fathers may be uncomfortable when milk leaks or sprays from the breasts during orgasm. (The hormone oxytocin is released during orgasm and is responsible for the spasmodic muscle contraction of the uterus during orgasm. Oxytocin also is responsible for the let-down reflex, and during orgasm, most nursing mothers' milk lets down.)

If you're uncomfortable about having your breasts fondled during sex while you're breastfeeding, or if the milk leakage or spray interrupts your sexual activity, talk to your partner about your feelings. One way to make sex more comfortable is to wear a bra with absorbent breast pads during sex. Though wearing a bra also may feel odd at first, some nursing mothers find that it is preferable to worrying about leaking or being uncomfortable about having their breasts manipulated during sex. Another way to minimize milk leakage is to nurse before you have or intend to have sexual relations.

Often, the nursing mother's sensitivity about her breasts and their nursing vs. sexual importance eases after she's become experienced at breastfeeding. Likewise, the father becomes less uncomfortable with breast milk leakage as he becomes more accustomed to his partner's role as a nursing mother. Thus, the use of a bra during sex or last-minute breastfeeding may be only a temporary measure during the period of adjustment both for the mother and father.

THE SENSUOUS NATURE OF NURSING

If your breasts have always been a sensitive erogenous zone, you probably will experience some sexual feelings while you are nursing. Some women experience some clitoral stimulation felt as a tingly tug that seems to stem from the baby's suckling. They experience some vasocongestion of their genitals and may begin to feel the wetness they usually associate with arousal. A few nursing mothers report that they've experienced orgasm while nursing.

The fact that breastfeeding is arousing for some women only makes sense. Most of you are accustomed to breast manipulation as a part of foreplay and intercourse. Some women have attained orgasm just from extensive breast manipulation. This link between arousal and breast manipulation doesn't cease to exist while you're nursing. However, the feelings of arousal you experience are likely to be altered by the context of the relationship you have with your infant. Instead of a heady, lusty, intense sexual experience, the arousal is more likely to lead to feelings of satisfaction and contentment. Most women report a deep sense of fulfillment from the stimulation rather than a tense, charged excitement that they associate with sexual arousal.

The sexual overtones of nursing are a well-kept secret in society. Because many of you will not expect to feel stimulated during nursing, you may feel guilty and horrified about the sensations you associate with nursing. Some women even stop nursing for fear that they're beginning a perverse relationship with their children. It's important for you to realize that many women become sexually aroused while nursing. It's a normal response and nothing to be ashamed of.

SENSORY CHANGES

Sex after birth may not be the same as sex before birth. It may feel just as good, but some of the stimulation that was pleasurable before may not seem to be on the mark afterward. A great deal of physiological alteration occurs during pregnancy and childbirth. Some women find their breasts are more sensitive, and some find them less so. Some find different areas of their genitals are more sensitive to stimulation. Some desire more foreplay and others will find intercourse more satisfying than before. Couples may have to explore new positions and new types of arousal techniques better suited to the mother's postpartum body. Such experimentation is hardly a bad influence on the sex life of most new parents. In fact, it can revive a sex life that had become too automatic and dull before pregnancy.

INTERCOURSE TUNNEL VISION

Intercourse often is difficult for the new mother for weeks or even months following birth due to a variety of the reasons outlined above. Rather than finding other ways of mutually satisfying sexual needs, many couples focus anxiously on the lack of coitus. Often the mother feels pressured to resume sexual relations before she's ready, and the father feels that his emotional and physical needs are being completely eclipsed by the new baby.

In narrowing their focus to this specific act, however, new parents forget the many other expressions of intimacy available to them when sexual intercourse isn't practical or desirable by one partner. Foreplay followed by manual or oral manipulation to orgasm can be a satisfying alternative to intercourse. This might be a time to try exotic creams or oils, new kinds of foreplay, and a variety of different positions that you might not have explored before. For the partner who desires physical closeness without engaging in the sexual act itself, using one of these options provides an opportunity for snuggling without the pressure to have sex. And the partner who desires intercourse may find that this new kind of sexual activity is even more exciting than what he or she was accustomed to. In fact, using ingenuity for sexual entertainment when intercourse is unavailable may turn out to enrich your postpartum love life permanently.

New mothers also may find masturbation to be an important part of regaining their sexual footing following birth since they can explore themselves and their sexual responses privately without having to be concerned about their partner's needs for the moment. When sexual relations are renewed, the new mother will know better how to tailor lovemaking to fit her postpartum sexual needs.

KEEPING THE BABY QUIET

Scientists may not have documented it, but *you* know that your baby has radar, a sixth sense, or some third eye out of which he or she can sense when Mommy and Daddy are finally close together. Here are some common tricks used by parents to keep the baby quiet and amused during your private moments:

- By far the most successful seems to be the baby-in-the-swing-turned-away-from-the-parents. Baby swings usually have a fifteen-minute wind-up capacity, but you often can purchase an extender that will keep the swing going for a half hour or longer.
- Put the baby in his or her crib with a long-running wind-up mobile, a mirror, and a rattle.
- Give the baby some juice in a bottle in the crib with the mobile wound up.
- Bring the baby for a visit to a neighbor's or relative's house for an hour.

THE FAMILY BED

The controversy still rages over the psychological implications of parents having sex with their baby in the same bed or room with them. Some experts say that an infant waking undetected in the bed and witnessing their parents in the throes of passion will be traumatized. Other experts feel that an infant won't be affected. Since no clear answers are available, your best bet is to discuss the psychological implications of the family bed with your pediatrician.

The psychological issues, however, are not the only ones that need to be addressed. Your physical needs also will become an issue. If your infant is a light sleeper, you may be the one who is traumatized by having your love-making interrupted frequently when your baby wakes up in bed and demands attention. Also, the newborn who sleeps where he or she is put in the early months of life can become a rock 'n roller in the second half of the first year of life and make sleeping accommodations very tight and uncomfortable. Trying to move a six month old out of your warm comfortable bed into the isolation of a crib may not be easy.

One option to the family bed you might want to consider is to put a futon (Japanese bed) or other mat on the floor next to your bed. Then, if you feel the need to comfort your baby during the night, you can lie down next to him or her on the mat for a while and return to your own bed afterward. Your baby will begin life sensing that you are nearby and available but that you have separate sleeping areas. The move to a separate room and crib may not be as difficult after this early sleeping rule has been established.

SUSAN
BEFORE HER WALKING ROUTINE

I can't believe you. You're such a *schtarker* (Yiddish word meaning something like strong as an ox). Where do you get the energy to swim half a mile? No thanks, I get as much exercise as I need turning the pages of a book with my thumb.

SUSAN
AFTER BEGINNING HER WALKING ROUTINE

Are you ready? Let's go. I don't want to talk too much because I find I need to concentrate to keep up my speed. This is great. It really gets me going. And you know what the best part is? I get a free half-hour in the morning. Before anyone has a chance to wake up and ask or cry for something, I'm out the door and in the park.

DAPHNE

I was really motivated to get back into shape after I had my baby. As a matter of fact, a year after Lucien was born, I was in the best shape I'd ever been in my life. I started exercising after about two months. I was still tired, and the class was hard for me, but I looked forward to getting out of the house and doing something for myself. It was a gift to myself, and that above everything else was what I needed. If you can just think about yourself for a little bit, it really helps you come back and want to give more to your baby.

10

GETTING BACK INTO SHAPE

Exercise is an important part of your postpartum recovery whether or not you are interested in becoming physically fit. Every postpartum woman needs to strengthen her abdominal muscles, her back muscles, and her pelvic floor muscles, which have been stretched and/or weakened during pregnancy and birth.

ABDOMINAL MUSCLES

Your abdominal muscles form a corset around your trunk running top to bottom from breastbone to pubic bone, side to side around your waist, and diagonally over the hips and down to the pelvis. These muscles are used in just about every effort you consciously and unconsciously make during the day, e.g., breathing, coughing, sneezing, bowel elimination, and bending or twisting from the waist in any direction. These muscles also help support the organs in the trunk and pelvis, the back, and, along with the buttock muscles, control the tilt of the pelvis.

During pregnancy your abdominals stretch enormously to accommodate your growing uterus. The stretch is so great that the two connected sheaths of muscles running from breastbone to pelvis (the recti abdominis) often separate. After birth, your abdominal muscles feel soft and jellylike. Their weakness may first be noticeable to you

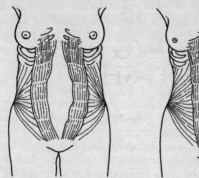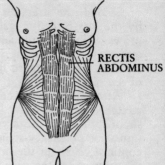

RECTIS
ABDOMINUS

**ABDOMINAL MUSCLES
SEPARATED IN LATE
PREGNANCY AND IMMEDIATELY   ABDOMINAL MUSCLES IN
AFTER BIRTH   NORMAL POSITION**

during your trips to the bathroom in the hospital, when you are unable to use your stomach muscles to assist in elimination. Sitting up also is difficult, requiring the added leverage of both arms where none was needed before pregnancy. The most obvious signs of the loss of muscle strength in the abdomen are the lack of any waist and the protruding belly, which makes you look as if you were five months pregnant instead of six weeks postpartum.

BACK MUSCLES

During pregnancy, your back is affected in two ways that make you more prone to back pain: First, the ligaments are softened (as are the ligaments of the pelvis and the rest of the body's skeletal structure) by progesterone and relaxin, two hormones. The softening prepares the pelvis to expand during birth. In other joints of the body, like the back, however, the softening results in a greater risk of injury since the ligaments provide a more flexible but weaker support for joints. In order to accommodate your changing center of gravity, you might unconsciously accentuate the normal curve in your lower back, causing a strain on the already compromised joint system.

Second, the stress on your back is further aggravated by the loss of abdominal muscle support as your uterus grows. The back muscles, unnaturally shortened by the increasing curve in the spine, become prime targets for strain as they are taxed more and more with the support of the spine for which they were not intended.

After birth, the abdominal muscles, although not stretched so greatly any longer, are not strong enough to support the back. Also, you might unconsciously fall back into your pregnancy stance even after birth, which would continue to strain the muscles in the back. And finally, the strength of the back ligaments continues to be compromised for five or six months until the effects of relaxin and progesterone wear off. These three conditions provide fertile ground for the development of chronic back pain.

PELVIC FLOOR

Most of the dirty little secrets about life after birth (leaking urine, flabby vagina, poor anal sphincter control over flatulence) that were alluded to but never explained by your mothers or grandmothers are the result of weakening of the pelvic floor.

The pelvic floor is a sling of muscles running between the front and back of your pelvis and forming a muscle hammock between your legs. This hammock supports the bowel, uterus, and bladder (see illus. pg 42). Three circular sphincter muscles incorporated in the hammock form the entrance to the internal passages leading to these organs, thus the strength of the pelvic floor not only affects the position and support of the bowel, uterus, and bladder but also control over the sphincter muscle openings and internal passages leading to them.

During pregnancy, many forces adversely affect the strength of the pelvic floor, culminating in the tremendous stretching and often tearing or cutting that the muscles are subject to during birth. The pelvic floor supports the increased weight of your uterus during pregnancy and then thins out and stretches to allow for the birth. It is subject to tremendous pressure as you bear down to deliver your baby.

After birth, the muscular hammock often sags and lacks resilience. The repaired tears or incisions are swollen and heal into inflexible scar tissue that takes many months to regain elasticity and strength. In this weakened condition, the pelvic floor doesn't support the internal organs properly and the sphincter muscles seem slack and lack good control. The weakness demonstrates itself in lack of control over the passing of gas, leaking of urine when pressure is applied to the pelvic floor, as when you laugh, cough or sneeze, and a flabby entrance to the vagina.

The weakness caused by pregnancy and birth will not be corrected by the natural healing process of the body. Your body may compensate as best it can for the lack of muscle support in the abdomen and pelvis, but you will remain at risk for disorders related to the muscle weakness, such as chronic backache and stress incontinence. These annoying and sometimes painful conditions were considered an unfortunate and unavoidable effect of childbearing in past generations. However, today it is recognized that exercise can correct the muscle weaknesses caused by pregnancy and childbirth and prevent or at least improve related disorders.

POSTPARTUM EXERCISE PROGRAMS

Once you've gotten a clean bill of health from your doctor at your six-week postpartum office visit, you'll be free to begin exercising regularly. However, you may not feel up to a thirty-minute aerobic workout yet. Remember, you're still recovering from your delivery. Your energy reserves are fairly low. Also, even the mothers who maintained a fairly active lifestyle up until birth will be somewhat out of shape from the birth as well as from the hiatus from exercise.

During the first couple of months following your postpartum checkup, you might find that you don't have the energy to get back into aerobic-level exercise at all. You might like to exercise, but at a less intense level than you did before you were pregnant. A gentler exercise routine at this stage in your recovery is appropriate. Consider enrolling in an exercise class specifically tailored to your postpartum needs. Postpartum exercise classes are designed around the particular weaknesses in the postpartum body, e.g., the abdominals, back, and pelvic floor. The classes also are less strenuous than a regular aerobics or calisthenics class. They function as a transition workout that prepares you to resume or begin your regular exercise routine.

Postpartum exercise classes are offered by many health clubs, exercise studios, and YW or YMCAs. The facilities usually provide babysitting services while you exercise or allow you to keep tiny infants in the room nearby.

Choose your classes carefully. Ask about your instructor's background. Has he or she been trained in the specific exercise needs of the postpartum body? Beware of class instructors who try to push you beyond your limit. Don't be intimidated into trying something you're not ready for. Instead, pick another class with a different, less zealous instructor who lets you work at your own pace.

When the postpartum class ceases to be challenging, you'll probably be ready to return to a more rigorous exercise class. If you are joining a health club or exercise studio for the first time, take the same precautions you did when choosing your postpartum class.

HOME EXERCISE PROGRAMS

For new mothers who can't or don't want to enroll in a formal class, several at-home options for postpartum exercise are available. To correct the birth-related muscle weakness described above, you'll want to follow a specialized postpartum exercise program such as that described in Elizabeth Noble's *Essential Exercises for the Childbearing Year* (Houghton Mifflin, 1982) or *The Postnatal Exercise Book* by Barbara Whiteford and Margie Polden (Pantheon, 1984). *The Postnatal Exercise Book* even incorporates your baby into the exercise program, using him or her as resistance.

If exercising at home alone doesn't spark your enthusiasm, try to organize a mother and baby exercise hour at your house with two or three friends. You'll be killing three birds with one stone: (1) getting some exercise; (2) taking time to be with your friends; (3) starting a play group for your kids.

When you are feeling up to a more exacting exercise class, you'll find many alternatives for working out at home. Tune in to one of the many local morning exercise programs that are usually aired between six and eight in the morning. You and your partner may enjoy doing the routine together with your baby as spectator, or you may want to take turns using the baby as resistance in the same manner as you did during your postpartum routines.

Many books, records, tapes, and videotapes offer exercise programs for home use. One popular program that comes in all these forms is *Jane Fonda's Workout Series*. Her records, tapes, and videos are particularly suited to home group exercise because of her enthusiasm and energy as well as her good choice in musical accompaniment.

Some of these routines, including Fonda's, may be too rigorous for you to complete each sequence at first. Remember to stop whenever you feel too winded or when you feel pain. As you become more fit, you'll find that you can complete more and more of the program.

CARDIOVASCULAR CONDITIONING

These postpartum classes will improve your muscle strength but will not improve your cardiovascular condition. To improve your cardiovascular condition, you need to incorporate aerobic exercise into your fitness program. Aerobic exercise increases your heart rate and breathing for an extended period of time, between thirty and forty-five minutes usually. If practiced regularly over a period of time, this kind of exercise improves your cardiovascular condition. Swimming, running, bicycling, and walking are all excellent aerobic exercises. Walking is a favorite with mothers since it can be combined with your baby's daily strolls:

- Walk to your friend's house.
- Pick a supermarket or greengrocer a mile or so from your home to shop for incidentals if you need an objective to your walks.
- If you have a park with a measured route for runners marked off, you might take your stroller over the course every day.

If you are just starting out in a cardiovascular program, you'll need to know how to fashion a progressive program that will gradually bring you up to your target fitness level. One good guide is Dr. Kenneth H. Cooper's *Running Without Fear* (Evans, 1985).

No matter how you decide to increase your physical activity after your six-week checkup, make sure that you don't overstrain by jumping into a full workout routine all at once. You'll only end up sore and exhausted. Whatever impetus you might have had to get back into shape can be extinguished easily by a few overstrenuous workouts. Instead, start your exercise program gradually and increase your exertion as you feel able.

EXERCISE AND OSTEOPOROSIS

A little known reason to join the ranks of the physically fit is the strengthening effect certain exercises have on bones. Osteoporosis is a disease most frequently seen in elderly women, the result of which is a weakening of the bones leading to deformation and fractures and breaks. The stooped posture of many older women often is attributable to osteoporosis; the vertebrae of the spine become weakened and collapse, leading to increased curvature of the spine and stooped posture. Frequent hip and wrist fractures also are attributable to this disease.

The weakening of bones in old age as a result of loss of bone mass occurs in both sexes. However, because women start out with less bone mass than men, and because the hormonal effects of menopause exacerbate bone loss, women develop an acute loss of bone mass more often than men.

Weight-bearing exercise, such as running, walking, bicycling, or weight training, all are stresses on the skeleton, particularly on the hips and legs, and they cause the bones to thicken to accommodate the extra stress. This extra density helps the bone remain strong despite the loss of mass later in life as long as exercise is continued.

Non-weight-bearing exercise, such as swimming, does not encourage bone growth. If swimming is your favorite exercise, therefore, you might consider adding a daily walk or a weight-training routine to your exercise schedule.

POSTURE

Good posture is critical to a mother's well-being. Certainly, you have been exhorted since childhood to hold your back straight and head high if for no other reason than to look self-assured. However, as a new mother your physical comfort actually becomes contingent on your posture because a great part of your day now involves picking up, putting down, and carrying your baby and all the paraphernalia that goes with him or her, all of which are potential strains on your muscles, particularly in the back. While your back and stomach muscles are weak and your ligaments are softened after birth, proper posture will help reduce the strain on your back muscles and ligaments and prevent backache.

Poor posture often develops out of bad habit started in pregnancy. As was mentioned earlier, a heavily pregnant woman often deepens the curve in her back by tilting her pelvis back and thrusting her belly forward to compensate for the changing center of gravity. This stance strains the muscles and the ligaments of the lower back. After birth, the new mother might fall back into this poor posture out of habit.

Further aggravating an overstrained back is the habit most mothers have of carrying their babies on one hip. Thrusting your hip to one side causes your spine to twist and puts a strain on back muscles and ligaments. Carrying weight unevenly on one side of your body only increases the strain on the twisted spine.

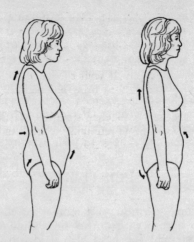

POSTPARTUM SLUMP   CORRECTED POSTURE

To prevent muscle strains, especially in the back, you need first to establish what good posture feels like. Stand sideways to a mirror. Look at your normal posture. Now, try this exercise. Imagine that someone has a string attached to the top of your head that runs straight through your body to your pelvis. Pretend that that string is being pulled straight up. First pull your head up, chin tucked in. Straighten your shoulders. Lift your chest slightly up and out. Pull in your stomach and tuck in your buttocks.

You have to admit, your mother was right.

This is great when you can stand in front a mirror, but how are you supposed to keep this perfect posture when you're doing two things at once all day, one of which usually is holding your baby? Here are some guidelines for keeping good posture:

•Invest in a baby carrier that can be adjusted so that the weight of your infant rests in the center of your chest. Make sure that the shoulder straps are well padded and that the waist or hip belt can be adjusted to fit snugly. When your baby is old enough to support his or her head, you might want to change to an adjustable backpack that puts the bulk of the weight high on your shoulders.

• When you buy a stroller or carriage, make sure that the handles are high enough so that you don't have to stoop to push it. If your choice is too low, invest in handle extenders to bring the handles up to the proper height.

• If you are used to bending from the waist to pick up whatever falls, begin retraining yourself to bend your knees when lifting packages or your child. The back muscles were not intended to assist in picking up heavy loads. Use your thigh muscles to get you up and down while holding your back straight and your load close to your chest.

JANET

When Jack was eight weeks old, I went back to work. Before I had a baby, there was nothing stopping me from working eleven-hour days at my job when I had to. And I didn't mind that. My job is very challenging and I love the work I do. However, when I returned to the office I knew I would have to go in at 9:00 and be out by 5:30. At first I was scared. How could I do a good job with such a strict schedule? Wouldn't I be too tired from working to be a good mother and too tired from mothering to be a good editor? The truth is that when I'm with Jack in the morning and he's at his most charming, I do regret giving him up to the sitter. I'm reluctant to leave him to go to the office. But at the end of the day the opposite is true. Often, I'm in the middle of something I'd really like to finish and I'm just as reluctant to leave the office as I was to leave home. What I'm trying to say, I guess, is that at the moment I'm feeling as if I can't get enough of either job to satisfy me, and I don't think that currently there's a solution to that problem for working women who want to have babies, too.

HEATHER

I went back to work after four months, so I had more time than most at home with my son. I did feel somewhat reluctant to leave Tucker even at that point. He still seemed so vulnerable. I found a good sitter, however, so I was confident that he was receiving good care. I tell you what eventually made up my mind to leave my job. I was seeing Tucker for an hour and a half or two hours a day. That's it. After spending all day and night with him, I scarcely had time to greet him coming and going from work. I would call the sitter and get secondhand reports about what he was doing. Sometimes I would sit in my office and cry after I got off the phone because I missed him so much. I just decided that Tucker was only going to be a baby once. I didn't want to miss him growing up. I didn't want to hear about his milestones from someone else. I wanted to be there.

11
WORKING

Many of you will be returning to work six to eight weeks after your baby is born. Few mothers return to a full-time job without conflicting feelings about leaving their babies so soon. Don't let colleagues make you feel that you're being overly sensitive about this separation. Leaving a two-month-old infant eight or ten hours a day is a wrenching experience. You may find yourself preoccupied with your baby's welfare, wanting to call your sitter several times a day to find out how things are going. You may even find yourself feeling a powerful sense of longing to be at home after a few hours on the job. These are all normal feelings for a mother whose life has been so intimately bound to her newborn's for the past six or eight weeks. In fact, experts in child development are lobbying now for a mandatory four-*month* leave for new mothers. They believe that at six or eight weeks the new mother is simply unprepared emotionally and often physically to be away from her newborn.

Of course, not every mother will feel bereft for the hours she is at work. Mothers who have a quick commute, a competent, reliable caregiver, a supportive work environment, and satisfying work often are eager to get back to the office.

DAYCARE

Competent daycare, more than any other factor, seems to be the key to making a working mother's life functional. There is no greater anxiety than feeling that your child is spending half of his or her day in the hands of an incompetent or neglectful sitter. Finding a regular, reliable sitter may take some time, so start your search right after you have your baby. A friend is probably the best source for a referral. If you hear of an extraordinary sitter who will be available when or even a little before you need her, pounce. Personally recommended caregivers come along infrequently.

Another principal source is domestic service agencies which screen applicants for you, so your chances of hiring competent, reliable help is greater than if you were hiring someone on your own. If you and the caregiver don't get on, the agency will offer you a replacement. However, this service can have a steep price tag that is impractical for many new mothers returning to work.

> Agencies can cause more aggravation than they save. If you decide to hire a sitter through one, get a few recommendations from other mothers, your pediatrician, or local parents' resource groups.

Hiring a sitter from a want ad is another possibility. Many people place a want ad in a community bulletin or local newspaper to find a caregiver. When you hire someone this way, get several recent references and check them out diligently. Also, depend on your instincts. Does the caregiver feel right to you? Do you like the way she approached and played with your baby? If someone has all the right answers to your questions but just doesn't click with you, you're better off looking elsewhere.

Make sure to give yourself enough time not only to interview sitters but to employ your candidate for a week or two before you return to work. You will have a chance to see how she handles the baby, whether she holds him or her frequently, whether she has any child care habits you disagree with (e.g., "propping" the bottle rather in the crib rather than holding the baby while feeding him or her), whether she is prompt, and whether, when you drop in after an errand, you find that your child is being cared for adequately in your absence.

If you are taking your baby to the sitter's home, ask for a tour of the house when you interview her. Aside from obvious signs of unsanitary conditions, look to see if the house is child-proof. Also, if the sitter takes care of any other children, take a look at how they seem to be faring. Ask for the names of a few references, including parents whose children are currently in her care. Here, again, bring your child to the sitter a week or two early and drop in to pick him or her up unexpectedly a few times to see if the sitter is as nurturing and competent in your absence as she appears in your presence.

> One way to determine if your baby is being held during the day is to see if the sitter's cologne (if she wears one) lingers on your baby's clothes when you return home.

NURSING AND WORKING

Nursing mothers who had planned on weaning when they returned to work often find that nursing provides a link with their newborn which eases the transition from full-time mother to working mother. While some mothers are fortunate enough to live close enough to work to run home midday to nurse, many more have schedules and/or locations that prohibit such an indulgence.

Nursing, fortunately, is a flexible activity. A mother's milk production in many instances can be modified to fit a working schedule. If you want only to nurse once in the morning and then again when you get home at night, you may be able to modify your milk production by skipping one feeding a day before you go to work and then eliminating a second feeding (if necessary) once you're on the job. At first, you may feel uncomfortably full during the day. Expressing a little milk to lessen the engorgement will help ease that full feeling as well as the tendency to leak. If all goes well, you should have the supply of milk that you need at night and in the morning without midday discomfort in a few days. However, some women find that their milk production slows down too much if they limit their nursing sessions to twice a day. If you feel that your milk supply is diminishing too much, you might want to follow the same instructions given in Chapter 5 for full-time nursing mothers who wish to build up their milk supply.

If a mother chooses to nurse full time when she's at work she can do so by expressing her milk at the times she normally would nurse at home. Many women find that the only private place they can find to express milk is in a bathroom stall, which is serviceable but not very aesthetically pleasing or physically comfortable. If you can, try to find an empty office or borrow a friend's office when he or she is on lunch or break at the times you need to express milk. Then use the method of expression with which you're most comfortable—either manual or pump—to express as much milk as possible from both breasts. Your manual or pump expression won't be as efficient as your baby, so leave plenty of time for expressing your milk. When you're finished, pour the milk into a storage container and either keep it in the office refrigerator/freezer until you go home or put it in your own insulated bag containing ice or a cold pack.

If you keep up your regular nursing schedule via expressing during work hours, you should have an adequate supply of milk to nurse fulltime on weekends or holidays when you have the whole day with your baby.

WORKING AND FATIGUE

If you are going back to work when your baby is two or three months old, chances are that he or she will not be sleeping through the night. You may still be up once or twice a night nursing or giving a bottle. Even if you share the duty with the father, you may find that the interrupted sleep on two or three nights of the work week takes a toll on you during the day. Many mornings you're tired by the time you get to work and half asleep by mid afternoon.

There's no magic palliative for the fatigue of the working new mother. The fact is that until you're getting a solid night's rest you're likely to be less than your spirited self during the day. However, some of the following ideas may be helpful in making your workday more pleasant and productive:

- Get up. Stretch your legs. Take a walk around the block if you can. If you have a desk job where you're facing a wall most of the day, a flash of sunlight, some fresh air, and a little exercise can rejuvenate you.
- Arrange your work schedule to take advantage of your most energetic moods. If you feel the effects of your lack of sleep most in the morning, try to do your routine work at that time and save the challenging work until later. If you seem to lose your ability to concentrate in the afternoon, make the opposite kind of schedule. If your energy tends to flag in late morning, pick up after lunch, and run out in the late afternoon, try to arrange meetings and your work schedule to follow your energy cycle.
- Keep in mind that the fatigue is temporary. Eventually, your child will sleep through the night—and so will you.

QUITTING

First of all, you are not the only new mother who has quit either at the end of her maternity leave or just after she's returned to work. *Many* new mothers feel that they and their babies are being cheated when they are away from home nine or ten hours a day. Many just can't find good daycare or are too distraught at leaving their helpless infant with a stranger. Others who return to work find themselves in tears on the phone when they get a second-hand report from the sitter of the baby's first attempt to hold something, clap hands, or roll over. They just don't want to miss these events that happen once in a lifetime to go through the daily grind at the office. They want to be home with their babies.

If you decide to leave your job, don't be surprised if you have some private moments of panic at the thought of leaving behind your professional identity for an undetermined period of time to devote yourself to motherhood. Feelings of ambivalence when giving up such a large part of your life are normal and probably compounded by today's social environment, which often seems more supportive of the working mother than the full-time mother.

One way to handle mixed feelings about leaving your job is to create a support group with other mothers in your area who have made the same decision. The support group will keep you from feeling and being isolated without the camaraderie of the office environment. You may also find, as time goes on, that the group provides a fertile environment for developing alternatives to full-time work, if you're interested in resuming a career. Some mothers may be able to pool their talents to start a business. When one mother is about to give up a part-time job to go to another, she may be able to pass the work along to someone else in the group.

In a real sense, this generation of American mothers returning to work so soon after birth are pioneers. Many of your decisions about combining motherhood with professional life will have to be based on your intuition about your individual situation rather than on any established guidelines. You have to make peace with yourself about the parts of your life that will have to be put aside while you scramble to manage career and motherhood. You also need to take time frequently to take stock of the balance you create to see if it is meeting your needs and your baby's. Often in the first few months of combining work and motherhood, adjustments need to be made in the schedule to make enough room for you, your baby, your job, and your partner in one day. You may have to wake up an hour earlier to get your exercise routine in or to have an extra hour with your baby. You may have to forgo elaborate cooking except for two nights a week in order to make time for a family hour. Regular lunches with your partner may become an important time to make contact with each other without the pressures of work or parenthood. However you decide to juggle working and motherhood, make sure to keep your priorities clearly in mind and address them before you attend to the less important matters in your life.

In the next nine months of motherhood, many of the disruptions in your daily life as well as the postpartum changes in your body will begin to fade from memory as you return more and more to your former physical and emotional state, and your baby develops more conventional eating and sleeping habits. Before you know it, your head will turn every time a mother with broad hips, a tired face and a nondescript bundle in a snuggly walks past you, and you may find yourself feeling relief or—believe it or not—longing.

FOUR TO
TWELVE MONTHS

DRAKE

Heather was invited away to a wedding for a weekend. I said, "Go ahead, Tucker and I'll 'bach' it." It was the first time I was totally in charge of him for a weekend, and we had a great time. I am familiar enough with his needs to know I can fulfill those needs on my own. It's true that after I went back to work Heather set up a schedule for him that I have had to learn about. But I insist on finding out how to do everything that she does for him. Tucker's very important to me, probably more important than anything else in my life has ever been. In light of that, I want to be in there taking care of him.

LESLIE

By the time six months had passed, I still had a few extra pounds on me. I was really tired of trying to squeeze into my old clothes, so I finally went out and bought clothes in a larger size. I look nicer in the larger clothes because they fit better, and I'm more comfortable, too. I don't know if I'm ever going to lose those last few pounds. But I feel good about myself now. I've been exercising regularly, which is something I haven't done in years, and my figure is in better shape because of it. The few extra pounds just don't bother me because I look and feel good.

DAPHNE

You know, it's funny. Two babies and five years later, I find that I've just gotten comfortable with my body. I took a look at myself in the mirror the other day, and my body's not perfect. I mean, I'm a little bent in the shoulder (which I'm trying to correct through exercise), there's a little extra skin on my belly, and my breasts are not as uplifted as they were before I had children, but it doesn't bother me so much anymore. It's important to look good, and I do as much as I can to stay looking good, but there are just some things you can't correct. I'll be damned if I'm going to sit here and feel self-conscious about my stomach or my breasts when I can't do anything about them.

12
BACK TO NORMAL

You probably haven't noticed it, but motherhood has become almost instinctive over the last year. Now when you're by yourself waiting for a bus, you sway slightly to and fro in the automatic comforting movement you used so often with your baby. You also have gotten the knack of being able to handle phone conversations, cooking, cleaning, and laundry while keeping your child in peripheral vision at all times. Your reflexes are legendary. You can practically leap the length of your living area in one bound when your baby is just about to bring down a lamp, pull a plug out of a wall, or fall off a chair he or she has managed to pull up on. And all of this is done automatically, without missing a beat in your conversation on the phone, in your preparation of a dinner for six, or whatever other activity you might be engaged in. You've truly incorporated motherhood into your life.

While you've become more adept at being a mother, your newborn has become more adept at being a baby. No longer the compliant tiny person so dependent he or she still seemed tethered to you by some visible umbilical cord, your baby now has some sense of self—of likes, dislikes, and ways to avoid the latter and win the former. You probably feel less as if your baby is a physical extension of yourself. He or she seems to be functioning so independently compared to just a few months ago.

As your baby nears the first birthday, you may feel some nostalgia for the time when he or she could be comforted so easily just by being rocked in your arms. However, you're probably also feeling a renewed sense of independence. You finally can sit alone with your partner at the dinner table without being interrupted every other minute for some detail of newborn care. You can drop your robust nine or twelve month old at the sitter and not be haunted as you leave for work that your fragile newborn will somehow come to harm without your protective attention. Your sleep is probably interrupted less often, so you have more energy to devote to work and motherhood. Finally, both jobs are beginning to be enjoyable. You're starting to feel like your old self again.

Nursing mothers often wean during this time, breaking their last physical link with their babies and allowing their bodies to return to a normal cycle. Mothers who have had a steady weight loss usually find themselves within a few pounds of their original weight. And most mothers suddenly realize that their waists and hips have some shape again. Collarbones that disappeared under a layer of fat reappear to cradle a favorite necklace. Wrists and hands are slim and elegant again. The impossible seems to be happening. You're beginning to look and feel the way you did before you had a baby, albeit with a few lingering reminders of the tumultuous experience of pregnancy and childbirth.

WEANING

Many women find that the period between six and twelve months presents a natural weaning time. The baby is likely to have started eating whole foods and so will be demanding less milk from you, and by the end of the year he or she probably will be able to tolerate cow's milk unless some allergy is present. Mother's milk, while still a healthy part of the baby's diet, doesn't provide the perfect diet for the baby any longer.

Sometimes a mutual weaning takes place where the mother and the baby seem less interested in nursing and gradually shorten and eliminate feedings. In other situations, however, the mother is more interested in weaning

than the baby or vice versa. The person who is not ready
to stop breastfeeding will undoubtedly suffer some feelings of frustration and sadness, but if weaning is done
slowly and compensated for with lots of physical contact,
then it shouldn't prove too traumatic for mother or baby.

When you're ready to wean, pick the shortest nursing
of the day when your baby seems most distracted by
other more interesting things and eliminate that feeding.
Try having your partner spend some time with your son
or daughter during that time—especially if it's a meal—so
that he or she won't get the regular signals that a nursing
time is approaching. By this time, you're probably producing less milk than when your baby was depending on
you completely for nourishment, so you shouldn't be
uncomfortably engorged by skipping just one feeding. If
you do become uncomfortable toward the time for the
next feeding, you can express just enough milk to ease the
pressure. However, don't overdo the expressing, as that
will signal your breasts to increase production of milk—
just the opposite of what you want to happen.

When you and your baby have become accustomed to
the loss of one feeding, pick another one that seems of
little interest and drop that one next. Continue in this
manner, dropping one feeding at a time after the adjustment is made, until you're down to just one or two
feedings a day. You'll usually be left with the morning or
night feeding or both. These are the hardest for both
mother and baby to give up, and they're also the most
convenient feedings to maintain. Thus, if you and your baby
want to enjoy these intimate nighttime and morning rituals, don't feel rushed to end them. During the time you
are enjoying these last feedings, however, you might want
to institute other rituals that will have the same comforting effects on your baby. Maybe your partner can become
more active in the nighttime ritual and make bathing,
story reading, and a lullaby an alternative to nursing to
sleep. Mornings could be spent with a few minutes of play
in Mommy's and Daddy's bed before everyone gets on
with the day rather than at Mommy's breast in a rocking
chair. You'll find that there are many ways to make weaning
less a withdrawal of intimacy than a transition to other

kinds of physical and emotional closeness between you and your child.

After you've finished weaning, you may be surprised to see that you still do produce a small amount of milk for many months. Sometimes you might notice a few drops leaking during a shower or during sex. Milk production does continue at a very low level for some time after you wean and takes anywhere from several weeks to several months to stop completely, depending on the woman.

EMERGENCY WEANING

If for some reason you have to stop nursing abruptly, you and your baby might have a more difficult adjustment to weaning. While some babies who are used to the bottle don't fuss too much at losing their breastfeeding privileges if they're given the same amount of cuddling that they're used to, others pull at their mothers' shirts and wail in frustration when they are not offered the breast. You also may feel saddened when suddenly you are cut off from your close moments with your baby and when you are deprived of the gratification of nourishing your baby directly. After all, nursings may be the only times during the day when you are forced to sit still and spend some time really focused on your baby rather than trying to keep him or her out of trouble while you're busy doing something else. Within that observation, however, lies a source of comfort for the sense of loss that you may feel when you're forced to wean prematurely: Keep those regular periods of interaction the baby. Read stories, play games, sing songs, take walks, but don't give up the time you give your baby just because you have to give up nursing.

If your weaning is abrupt, your emotional distress might be complicated by physical discomfort when your breasts become engorged and are not emptied of milk. Don't punish yourself by suffering through the engorgement. You can express enough milk to ease the discomfort without encouraging greater milk production if you express only enough to relieve the sense of pressure.

PHYSICAL SHAPE

Many women find that although they weigh the same as they did before they were pregnant, their clothes don't fit the same and their bodies don't look the same. Some common observations are the following:

CHANGE IN WEIGHT DISTRIBUTION Sometimes weight distribution changes. The bust may be a little larger. Hips and waist may retain a thickness that makes the tight jeans and skirts from before pregnancy *too* tight for comfort despite your being back to your original weight.

BREASTS If you didn't breastfeed, you might be pleasantly surprised at the way your skin is beginning to firm up around your deflated breasts at the end of this year. However, for women who are still nursing or who weaned in the last half of the year, the skin is going to take some time to regain some tone. Don't be dismayed if your breasts look like flattened pancakes right after you wean. They may not return to their original fullness, but they probably will become substantially more uplifted than they appear right after you finish nursing.

Some new mothers put themselves through rigorous exercise programs meant to lift and firm their breasts back to their original shape. Exercise can help strengthen and firm your pectoral muscles, which may give a bit more lift to your bust, but no exercise will shrink the skin of your breasts back to its original size if you grew two or three sizes larger than normal during pregnancy.

You shouldn't feel, however, that just because your breasts are shaped differently than they were before that they are unattractive. Breasts don't grow in one perfect form. They develop in as many shapes and sizes as there are women. Maybe your breasts look different and unfamiliar to you, but they probably are as attractive in their new shape as they were in their old. You'll be less self-conscious about their new shape as you grow accustomed and comfortable in your postpartum body.

WAIST   Your waist was probably the first feature of your figure to disappear after you became pregnant. As you saw it stretch so far out of shape to accommodate your growing baby, you probably thought that your prized wasplike figure was lost forever. However, many women find that their waists snap back into shape by the end of the first year if the pregnancy weight has been lost. The skin around the waist and the stomach and waist muscles may not be as taut as before, however, so a little roll may form over the waistband where one didn't before. In time, the skin will regain more of its tone, and exercise can help tighten the muscles of the abdomen.

HIPS   Rumor has it that your hips are permanently expanded after childbirth. The rumor, however, is false. The pelvic bones don't stay permanently widened after birth, but the extra layer of fat and loose muscles that cause the hip spread certainly *do* seem permanent to most new mothers even a year after birth.

Fat that layers the hips seems to be the most resistant to weight reduction in women. Many new mothers find that long after they've fit back into their old T-shirts and full skirts, their pants still are unattractively tight around the hips. You may just want to buy the next size larger pants if your weight is slightly higher than before but still within the normal range for someone of your height and size. There's no rule that you *must* fit into your pre-pregnancy clothes to be attractive again. For some women, the added weight may round out a formerly boyish figure and give them a feminine figure they've always wanted. For others, the extra padding may be unnoticeable except to their own overly critical eye. If you look good to yourself without your clothes on and the only detraction from your satisfaction with your figure is the fact that you can't pour yourself into your size five jeans, maybe it's the jeans rather than the last couple of pounds that should go.

For those of you who are hellbent on trimming down your hips, remember that starvation diets aren't the answer. Regular exercise that strengthens and firms the hip muscles will be much more effective.

SKIN PIGMENT CHANGES

Many of the pigment changes that occur during pregnancy are longlasting or even permanent. The most common areas of the body affected by pigment changes are the face, nipples and aureola, linea nigra, and labia.

FACE If you developed the mask of pregnancy (brown [for fair complexions] or white [for dark complexions] spots on your face, neck, or abdomen) you've probably noticed that the pigmented areas have faded considerably since childbirth. In some women, the spots disappear entirely, but others notice that a faint shadow of the mask (usually unnoticeable to everyone but the mother) remains for months or even years. If you are self-conscious about this faint coloration on your cheeks, you can use a light foundation to conceal it.

NIPPLES AND AUREOLA These usually are enlarged and much darker during pregnancy. As your breasts get smaller, your aureolas may seem larger in relation to the rest of your breast than before. Their color, which can deepen to dark brown in olive- or dark-complexioned women, will lighten somewhat but probably will not return to the shade they were before pregnancy.

LINEA NIGRA Very fair pregnant women may develop only a pale pink line up the middle of their abdomen during pregnancy, but darker-complexioned women often notice a much darker linea nigra. After birth, the pigmented line will begin to fade, but many months may have to pass before the line disappears altogether. Some women notice a faint shadow of the linea nigra from their navel down to their pubic bone even years after birth. Again, it is most apparent to the mother herself, so don't be shy about wearing a bikini if it's your habit to do so. No one else will be able to discern the faded shadow of your linea nigra.

LABIA   While your outward appearance won't be affected by the deepening of the color of your labia, you might be surprised if you do a self-examination to find that the pink folds of skin are now maroon-colored. This change in color of the labia following pregnancy is normal, however, and no cause for alarm.

CESAREAN INCISION SCARS

Don't be disturbed if your incision scar is still a dark red at the end of your first year of motherhood. Scars often take several years to fade to a slighty pink, barely noticeable line. You might be concerned to see that yours is fading much more slowly than a friend's or a sister's, but remember that variation in postpartum recovery is the rule rather than the exception. Your body is repairing itself at a rate that is appropriate for you.

STRETCH MARKS

Some women swear that they didn't develop stretch marks because they religiously massaged themselves with coconut cream or aloe cream or both. Unfortunately, neither of these creams nor any other measure is known to prevent stretch marks—those red, spiderlike blemishes that usually develop during pregnancy as the skin stretches. You can be comforted to know that over time the stretch marks will fade to normal skin tone, though many have a silvery sheen to them.

SKIN TAGS

Some of you may have grown these little flaps during pregnancy. Most often, they appear on the neck, under the arms, or on the breasts. The tags will remain after birth. The tags don't pose a health problem, but if you are embarrassed by them, consult a dermatologist about having them removed.

VARICOSE VEINS

Varicose veins—swollen veins that may appear as a slightly raised vessel running down the legs or as a bulging purple clump of vessels—are caused by the pressure on the legs from the enlarging uterus as well as by the increased fluid being pumped through the circulatory system during pregnancy. Whether or not you develop varicose veins during pregnancy has more to do with your heredity than with what kind of stockings you wear. Varicose veins usually look much worse than they feel. Some women complain of heaviness or fatigue in the legs. If the veins are greatly swollen, they may cause an aching after long periods of standing.

If you did develop these enlarged veins during pregnancy, you've probably noticed a great improvement in them since you gave birth. Remember, however, that the veins are permanently weakened and therefore more prone to becoming varicose in the future. To prevent this condition from worsening:

- Wear support hose if you're going to be on your feet a great deal. This will help support the veins.
- Exercise to promote good circulation in your legs.
- Break up long periods of sitting by getting up and stretching out your legs.
- When you sit down, try to elevate your feet so that your heels are above your hips. This will keep the blood from pooling in the weakened vessels.

Varicose veins can be removed surgically, but this drastic measure should only be considered if the veins are considered a threat to your health.

INCREASED MUCUS PRODUCTION

Some postpartum women notice that they produce much more vaginal lubrication and cervical mucus than they did before they had a baby. This is a normal development and nothing to worry about. Usually, the extra mucus is welcome as it makes sex more enjoyable.

As mothering takes up less of your mental energy, many of you may begin thinking about going back to work—if you haven't already—or taking your life in a different direction altogether from what you were doing before you gave birth. Now that you've had some distance from it, maybe your profession doesn't seem as rewarding as you'd like it to be. A change in jobs or careers might be in order. Or perhaps motherhood is so enjoyable that you decide to put off work altogether so that you don't have to give your babysitter the richest part of the day with your child. However you decide to combine your new role as mother with your other roles, make sure that you make a plan that is comfortable for you rather than one that fits into society's current lifestyle fashion. Unfortunately for new mothers, many people seem to be ready to tell you what you absolutely must do for the health of your baby and yourself—even if "what you must do" would make you unhappy. Your best bet is to tune into your own feelings and discuss the pros and cons of your plans with your partner or trusted friends who won't push you into a prefabricated role that doesn't fit.

One of the desires that might begin to take shape now is to have another baby. That idea certainly will draw a torrent of unwelcome horror stories and caveats that prob-ably aren't relevant to you. However, what you should consider is whether or not you're ready to become preg-nant again. In the following chapter, you'll find some guidelines for preparing for a second pregnancy.

INARA

At six months postpartum: Are you kidding? No sir. One is enough for me. I'm just barely beginning to feel like a human again. Seriously, I like Pauli now that he's a little older. Newborns really don't do that much for me.

INARA

At eighteen months: Well, if I had another baby (I'm not thinking about it, though), I'd have a scheduled C-section so I wouldn't have to go through all the torture and then end up with a C-section anyway. That's for sure.

SAUL

Inara's husband, at two years: We think we're pregnant.

SHARON

Eighteen months after her second child: I had two children, both by Cesarean section. Two really was all I wanted. But when Elisabeth grew into the large size diapers and wasn't an infant anymore, I started thinking about having a third baby. Another tiny newborn to cuddle. I really had to snap myself out of it and remind myself that all newborns turn into babies and then into toddlers and eventually into adults. You never can have an infant for as long as you'd want. Babies are like kittens. They grow up too fast. But I have to remember that infancy is ephemeral and having more babies isn't going to make it last longer.

13

GETTING READY FOR THE NEXT BABY

Most of you were told that the love for your newborn is so great it immediately wipes out all memory of pain experienced during labor and overrides your exhaustion and irritation in the early months of motherhood. Most of you now know that's not true. Memories of childbirth today, often unblurred by drugs for most of the delivery, remain sharp for several months. And during the strain of those first months of motherhood, there *are* times when you want to throw the baby out with the bath water. At these times, any small gains made toward normalizing your life again strengthen your resolve never to put yourself through this trial again.

As the months roll by, however, the trial seems less gruesome. Your baby's not a baby anymore but a toddler able to amuse him or herself, play with other children, and happily stay with a sitter or neighbor until you get home from a night out with friends.

You also notice, however, that your toddler is hard to hold in your arms when you're trying to comfort him or her. Long legs dangle off your lap. An inquiring hand reaches past you for whatever's on the shelf behind the chair. Or maybe your toddler just isn't that interested in being rocked and comforted anymore. A quick hug and kiss will do, thank you. For many of you, it's these first signs of independence—these clear signs that your baby is no longer a baby—that cloud the memory of your early days as a mother with sentimentality. You remember dressing and nursing and rocking your tiny newborn with the wide eyes, toothless grin, and miniature hands and feet. You remember when the bathroom sink was too large a bathtub, when a dresser drawer was a kingsize bed for your newborn. And you remember the pride and thrill of holding your baby just after birth. Sure labor and delivery was hard, but what you really remember now is the wonder you felt looking at your newborn who—just out of the womb—was looking straight back at you. You'd like to experience that feeling again. As a matter of fact, you'd like to love and nurture someone else as much as you do your big boy or girl. Before you know it, you're telling yourself the same thing you did the first time you got pregnant, only with a little twist: "Look, millions of women have six, seven, even twelve children. It can't be *that* hard to have two."

When you decide to get pregnant a second time, you need to consider not only your emotional readiness but your physical readiness as well. Unfortunately, very little is known about what a woman can do to get into shape for the rigorous experience of pregnancy. Most of the specific information available about diet, exercise, and health habits is for the woman who already is expecting a child. Nonetheless, there are some general health considerations for you to keep in mind before you get pregnant.

THE BEST SPACE BETWEEN BABIES

When people talk about timing their pregnancies, they're usually trying to take into consideration their children's psychological health. Several years ago, three years was the recommended time. Now, some researchers suggest that spacing babies either one year or five years apart is better. They also admit, however, that there is no formula for stress-free family planning. Each child will react differently to his or her new sibling, depending on the child's emotional makeup. Jealousy and rivalry may be enhanced by age-related emotional reactions, but they're almost certain to arise in some form regardless of how many months or years you wait. That's a much needed reassurance for the large number of new mothers in their mid-thirties to early-forties who can't wait five years between children but also can't take on the emotional and physical burden of planning their children one year apart.

What's the best time to plan your second child then? When you're feeling physically and emotionally ready to take on the job of mothering two children. The following list covers some common considerations that mothers should keep in mind when thinking about having a second child:

Do you feel good? If you still feel tired all the time as well as emotionally overextended, you should talk to your practitioner before trying to get pregnant a second time. Some of you may have become so accustomed to feeling exhausted all of the time that you think it's the normal postpartum state. However, after your baby is weaned and sleeps through the night, you should be feeling as vigorous as you did before your first birth. If you don't, you need to look for the cause of your fatigue and remedy it before taking on another pregnancy and another infant. Pregnancy is a rigorous experience and requires you to be in optimum physical and emotional health.

Have you treated conditions that arose during the first pregnancy? Hemorrhoids, back problems, stress incontinence, and any other pregnancy-related disorder should be controlled by the time you begin your second pregnancy.

Is your relationship with your partner strong? Many times, the stress of having a child takes a toll on a relationship that may go unnoticed until the infant stage is over. Suddenly when the toddler is off in a corner playing by him or herself, the parents find themselves sitting in awkward silence, unable to find anything to talk about but the baby.

If you find that some of the closeness between you and your partner has been lost, now is the time to make a special effort to begin that intimacy before you become pregnant again. Make a special effort to get out once or twice a week. An occasional weekend alone also is a good idea. You want to start off your second with the sure emotional footing you had during your first pregnancy.

Have you solved your daycare dilemmas? You'll probably be depending ever more heavily on your caregiver as your pregnancy progresses and certainly after your newborn comes home. If you're hanging on to a daycare situation that is less than adequate just to avoid the frustrations of looking for someone or someplace new, you should look now for a new sitter or daycare that meets your needs. The little frustrations you put up with now may become insufferable when you're juggling two children.

> If you are changing your first child's daycare situation, make the transition as early on in your pregnancy as possible. You don't want your firstborn contending with a new caregiver at the same time he or she is adjusting to a new brother or sister.

Most doctors suggest waiting at least a year between pregnancies to let your body recover completely postpartum, but the majority of women don't really feel ready until after that time in any case.

UNREALISTIC EXPECTATIONS

Maybe the first time you got pregnant it was an accident. Maybe you really didn't try and you conceived in the first month. If you became pregnant effortlessly the first time, try *not* to count on the same thing happening the second time. Timing of conception is incredibly variable. Many women who conceived right away the first time take a year or more to conceive the second time. A number of factors can delay the second conception.

First of all, your chances of getting pregnant do not improve after each pregnancy. In other words, the average time it takes to get pregnant remains six months whether you've one or six children. You might be on the short end of the spectrum—conceiving in one month—the first time, and on the long end of the spectrum—conceiving in more than six months—the second time.

The six-month average for conception is based on statistics for a man and woman in their mid-twenties who have sexual intercourse an average of three times a week. The average length of time for a couple in their mid-thirties with a new baby having sex once a week if they're lucky would be much longer. The less intercourse you have, the less chance you have to become pregnant.

You will be older when you conceive your second child, and depending on your age, that factor can influence your chances of becoming pregnant rapidly. Women in their twenties usually ovulate during every menstrual cycle, giving them twelve times a year to become impregnated. However, as they grow older and approach menopause, the number of anovulatory cycles (menstrual cycles where ovulation doesn't occur) increases. In your thirties, you might only ovulate nine or ten times a year, which would also reduce your odds of becoming impregnated in any given period of time.

The important message to keep in mind when you put aside your contraceptives, then, is that conceiving the second time may take a few extra months because of lifestyle changes or age-related changes. In the majority of cases, the length of time needed to conceive is no indication that the couple has an infertility problem.

WHEN TO GO FOR HELP

If you conceived once, usually you'll be able to become pregnant a second time with the same partner. However, in rare instances, you could have had some physical trauma after your first birth that may have led to second-child infertility. Also, you may have had interim infections or gynecological complications that could adversely affect fertility. Examples of medical conditions that might lead to second-child infertility are: (1) postpartum infection with damage to the Fallopian tubes and postpartum bleeding necessitating a D and C following birth, which may lead to scarring in the uterus and inadequate build-up of the uterine lining to sustain a pregnancy; (2) untreated sexually transmitted disease, such as chlamydia; (3) abortion with post-abortal infection; (4) development of fibroids; or (5) development of low sperm count in the partner.

If you have been trying to conceive for six months without results, you should contact your doctor for a checkup just to be reassured that you are in good health, or to have suspicious symptoms examined. Unless there is reason to suspect a physical complication interfering with conception, an infertility workup probably won't be recommended until you have been trying in earnest to become pregnant for a year. This rule of thumb varies with the age of the patient. If you're in your twenties or early thirties, the timing would appropriate. However, if you are in your late thirties or early forties, a workup may begin as early as six months after trying unsuccessfully to conceive.

One interesting statistic to keep in mind is the following: The accumulated data on infertility indicate that if all of the couples seeking help for infertility were left untreated, *80 percent* of them would conceive within three years.

TRYING TOO HARD TO GET PREGNANT

Many mothers who were lucky enough to get pregnant effortlessly the first time try to fit their pregnancies the second time into a tight time schedule. This is particularly true of working mothers who plan out a work schedule allowing "x" number of weeks for tiredness and morning sickness and then count back a month or two to find the month that they *have* to get pregnant. Both partners feel under a great strain if this kind of schedule is planned. The father feels that he has to perform on cue as soon as the mother's temperature and mucus inspection suggests that she's fertile, and the mother feels compelled to conceive even though she really has no control over this part of her life. Both partners also may become frustrated and angry at their first child, who always seems to need attention at the wrong time. Although the parents might have been interrupted many times before, suddenly the intrusions take on much more significance if they occur during critical times during the mother's cycle.

When you decide to get pregnant again, it doesn't hurt to keep track of your cycle to know approximately what time of month you're most fertile. However, making sex an afterthought following a series of self-examinations, temperature monitorings, and calendar planning takes the enjoyment and romance out of lovemaking. Forget the clinical side of conception. Just put aside your contraceptive device and enjoy the rare privilege of spontaneous sex.

If you are a working mother trying to fit a second pregnancy in your career, try not to make your schedule too tight. To begin with, of course, you might not get pregnant until six or more months after you decide to have a second child. Secondly, your next pregnancy might not be like your first. You may be *more* comfortable and able to shoulder your normal responsibilities even longer than you did during your first pregnancy. However, you also may find that your pregnancy is more difficult and you have to cut back on your responsibilities somewhat as you progress toward your due date.

VAGINAL BIRTHS AFTER CESAREAN (VBAC)

VBACs currently are optional, even though they are recommended for most women who deliver by Cesarean the first time. Often times, the circumstances that necessitated a surgical delivery the first time will not be present during the second delivery, making a repeat Cesarean unnecessary surgery. Physicians are increasingly having to justify the need for repeat Cesareans. As the pressure grows on the medical community to allow a trial of labor following a C-section, scheduled repeat C-sections for second children will not be the rule but the exception.

The tradition of "once a C-section, always a C-section" started when the only type of incision used for Cesarean sections was the classical vertical cut in the upper uterine wall. The muscle fibers in this part of the uterus don't repair strongly, and obstetricians feared that the weakness would put the mother at too great a risk of uterine rupture during a subsequent labor. Thus, scheduled C-sections after the first birth became standard procedure.

The classical (vertical) uterine incision is still used today under extenuating circumstances. When a premature infant is delivered by C-section, the practitioner must cut into the body of the uterus because the lower section of the uterus has not developed yet. Also, the classical section allows a safer delivery of the premature infant.

When the practitioner has to do any difficult maneuverings of the fetus, he or she will need to use the classical incision in order to gain greater access to the baby. The lower segment incision provides just about as big an opening through which to deliver a baby as the vagina, whereas the classsical incision allows the practitioner literally to open up the uterus and lift out or turn around the baby.

Most Cesarean sections today are performed using a smaller, lower horizontal uterine incision called a lower segment, transverse, or low flap incision. The tissue in this lower area of the uterus repairs much more rapidly and stronger than the muscular tissue in the upper part of the uterus, therefore the risk of a uterine rupture is virtually nonexistent. The majority of women who undergo this kind of C-section will be able to labor and deliver vaginally in nine months to a year without any significant risk of uterine rupture.

Because of the rapid and strong repair of these C-sections, the need for repeat surgical delivery is based not on past history but on the progress of the current labor and delivery. Since every pregnancy and birth is different, your practitioner really can't tell you whether or not you'll need a Cesarean section before you begin your labor.

If you have had a classical incision, you are probably not a candidate for a VBAC. However, you can't tell what kind of uterine incision you had by looking at the scar on your abdomen. Abdominal incisions running vertically may be covering uterine incisions running horizontally, and vice versa. You *must* find out what kind of *uterine* incision you had before you can consider a VBAC.

DRUGS

You know from your first pregnancy that you shouldn't take any medications during pregnancy other than those approved by your doctor. However, certain medications taken *before* pregnancy can linger in the body for several weeks and may affect the developing fetus after you conceive even if you stopped the medication at the first sign of pregnancy. Therefore, it's wise to check with your doctor or your pharmacist about the safety of any drugs you may be taking *before* you try to get pregnant again. You may be advised to wait two or three months to ensure that a drug is completely cleared out of your system.

DIET

There is some evidence now that what you eat *before* you're pregnant is as important if not more important than what you eat while your pregnant. Researchers feel that the health of the egg that is being fertilized is a function of what you were eating up to the point of conception. While the health of the developing fetus certainly is linked to your diet while pregnant, the health of the egg at the time you conceive is dependent on what you were eating up to moment of fertilization. Thus, when you begin to think about conceiving a second time, you should review your diet and make sure you're incorporating enough of the four basic food groups every day (see Chapter 7). Most women who are menstruating monthly are borderline anemic because of their menstrual flow, so your iron intake should be increased to compensate for the cyclical ebb of iron.

For most of you, good nutrition does not mean loading up on supplements and super vitamins. You do need, however, to look back at the daily recommended nutrition guidelines in Chapter 7 and see to it that you're keeping your body primed with all of the nutrients it needs every day. The only women who need dietary supplements to correct a deficiency are those who lost enough blood during delivery to become anemic. These new mothers need to take an iron supplement for three months if they are bottlefeeding, or for as long as they are breastfeeding, since they will continue to lose iron while they are nursing.

WEIGHT LOSS

It's not mandatory, but most doctors feel that it's wise for you to return to a healthy weight (not necessarily the weight you were before your first pregnancy) before conceiving a second time. If you go into your second pregnancy with ten or fifteen pounds left over from your first, you may come out of the second pregnancy with that much more weight to lose on top of your pregnancy weight in order to return to a healthy weight.

Most of you have a weight at which you're comfortable and a slightly lower weight which is always your goal. If it's important for you to get down to your goal before you conceive a second time, do so. However, your comfortable weight—if it's a healthy weight for you—is probably an adequate weight loss to achieve.

Some of you who still have ten pounds to lose at the same time you want to begin your second pregnancy are finding the advice to lose weight at odds with the advice to maintain a healthy diet. You can do both:

•You can get all the nutrition you need on 1,200 calories a day if you eat carefully.
•You can increase your weekly exercise schedule in order to increase the number of calories you use. Remember, crash diets generally provide short-lived weight losses and long-term nutritional deficits. Increased exercise combined with a healthy diet is the only way to lose weight permanently.

REDUCE CAFFEINE INTAKE

Most doctors suggest that you cut down or eliminate caffeine altogether while you're pregnant. However, as you may have found out during your first pregnancy, the sudden elimination of caffeine from your diet can cause withdrawal symptoms such as headache, irritability, and tiredness. Now that you know you'll have to give up caffeine, you might as well wean yourself off the substance slowly in order to avoid the withdrawal symptoms. A gradual substitution of decaffeinated products for caffeinated beverages over a period of weeks is the most painless method of removing caffeine from your diet.

EXERCISE

If you were to concentrate on getting your body into condition for a pregnancy, you'd probably want to strengthen your abdominals, back muscles, and pelvic floor (the sling of muscles supporting the urethra, uterus, and bowel), which bore the brunt of your last pregnancy (see Chapter 10).

REPEAT OFFENSES

Conditions such as hemorrhoids, varicose veins, backache, and stress incontinence are aggravated by pregnancies and usually worsen slightly with every pregnancy.

Exercise certainly helps control these lingering conditions and minimizes them during pregnancy, but it can't completely rectify the wear and tear of carrying and birthing a child.

If you follow these simple suggestions, you can feel comfortable that you're doing everything currently suggested to prepare yourself for a safe pregnancy. What you may not be expecting, however is the greater appreciation of and deeper satisfaction gained from your second pregnancy. As one woman pregnant for the second time expressed it:

"I was happy when I was pregnant the first time. I felt good most of the time, but I can't say I really was emotionally involved. The process seemed to go on without my effort. At times I was irritated that it interrupted my usual schedule at work.

"Now that I know what my body creates during those nine months, however, I look at pregnancy another way. Every new sign of motherhood makes me proud and excited. I want to savor this unique, fleeting experience since I'm not sure I'll have a chance to be pregnant again. It's so special and so rewarding in a way that nothing else in life can match. Even the nausea was exciting because it heralded a coming birth."

CONCLUSION

When I sat down to write this book, my son was just one year old and I was just beginning to feel like a human being again. I knew I wanted more children but couldn't imagine when I'd feel moved to put myself through the rigors of a second pregnancy. Now, as I finish this book and review the early parts, I find that I'm actually nostalgic for those first few days after birth with my newborn. Life is rich and fulfilling now, but almost everything pales beside the thrill of birthing and nursing a baby as he or she emerges from the newborn's cocoon as an individual.

As you can tell, I've just gotten to the point where I'm replacing the elastic in my maternity pants and hoping that I'll be using them in the not too far future. This time, though, I look forward to motherhood without the anxieties I had before. I have learned from my experience and the experience of other new mothers how to make myself comfortable and enjoy early mothering.

It is my hope that this composite of hints, rules of thumb, well- and little-known remedies from mothers and obstetrical health care workers will give you the kind of information I lacked after the birth of my first child. I hope that you will understand why your body looks and feels the way it does so that you won't worry unnecessarily when well-meaning but misguided friends and relatives criticize (however constructively) your shape or weight or nursing style. And I hope that this understanding helps you feel more confident and relaxed in the early days of mothering so that you can savor the intimate moments with your newborn, because one thing other mothers will tell you is true: It *does* go by too quickly.

INDEX

ABOUT THE AUTHOR

Paula M. Siegel has been writing about women's health issues for more than a decade. She has written extensively on pregnancy, childbirth, and motherhood for many periodicals including *Redbook*, *Glamour*, and *Parenting*, for which she is a monthly columnist. The author has published two other books, including "Killing Pain Without Prescription" (Harper & Row).

Ms. Siegel divides her time between New York City and East Quogue, Long Island. She and her husband, Steve Duffy, have one son, William.